Cordially yours,
Anne Wertsner

MAKE YOUR OWN MERRY CHRISTMAS

MAKE
YOUR
OWN
MERRY
CHRISTMAS

BY

ANNE WERTSNER

DRAWINGS BY
LÉONIE HAGERTY

M. BARROWS
AND COMPANY, INC.
PUBLISHERS NEW YORK

Fourth Printing

PRINTED IN THE UNITED STATES OF AMERICA
BY J. J. LITTLE & IVES COMPANY, NEW YORK

To

THE MEMORY OF MY MOTHER AND FATHER

Who Loved Christmas Day

and

Carried Its Spirit Through the Year

Introduction

IN MY long, varied, and probably sometimes meddlesome career of horticultural contacts and garden experiences, I have not often seen things fit together so well as they did when I learned that Miss Wertsner was preparing a little book on home decorations entitled *Make Your Own Merry Christmas.* All her activities and experience in the years of my acquaintance made me feel that she could do this particular job exceptionally well, since she knows exactly what she is talking about.

For a number of years Miss Wertsner has served The Pennsylvania Horticultural Society, of which I happen to be Extension Committee chairman, as Field Secretary and Flower Show Director. She has also had wide experience and visited many gardens, not only in Pennsylvania but elsewhere. Many times the Society has had to "lend" her to other states wanting the kind of thing she teaches so well. She always served them with satisfaction, carrying progressive Pennsylvania thought to the states close to us, New York, New Jersey and Maryland, and also brought our ideas to many other states, Texas, Florida, Oklahoma, Louisiana, Connecticut, Massachusetts, West Virginia, Virginia, Ohio, and Illinois, to name a few.

Because I have watched her work and sometimes participated in what she was planning to write, I can heartily commend what she here has to say on making Christmas more vital through the use of the many decorations which are so readily available.

J. HORACE MCFARLAND

Breeze Hill, Pennsylvania

Foreword

The celebration of Christmas has two familiar and important aspects. Its real significance is religious, a festival kept with reverence by people of many faiths. But there is also the joy of Christmas. It is a time of jollity and good will, of family gatherings and happiness for children. Most grown people, aside from the spiritual meaning of the day, look at Christmas through the eyes of children. Its more familiar symbols, for both young and old, are Santa Claus, the tree, filled stockings, beautifully wrapped gifts, wreaths on the doors, holly, mistletoe and other decorations throughout the house. For nearly every American, these mean Christmas.

Then there are the customs of Christmas, borrowed from many lands and many ages. Carol singing, sleigh bells, yule logs, turkey, plum pudding, mince pies and cookies, crowded streets and stores, parties and merrymaking—these also mean Christmas in America.

Most people have hobbies. Stamp collecting, painting, fishing, gardening and a host of others fill the spare time of all sorts of people. It has been one of my own hobbies for many years to invent and make Christmas decorations. The idea is to devise decorations that are easy to make, not too expensive and yet effective. The elaborate adornments found in churches, stores and some stately homes at Christmas time are the work of highly-paid professionals; it costs a lot of time and money to produce them.

But the average American is likely to be short of both time and money at Christmas.

The season is a busy one for everybody. Shopping, addressing and mailing cards, gift wrapping, preparing cookies and fruit cake and special dishes take up a lot of time. It is extraordinary, in fact, how hard nearly everyone works in preparation for the holiday. It seems worth while to make, if we can, our own seasonal decorations quickly and at small expense. The time needed is little compared to what is required to prepare a dinner for many Christmas guests, and the decorations last much longer than the dinner.

Another argument for making your own is that the result will be, or should be, suitable to the size, character and color scheme of your home, which "store-boughten" decorations might not be. For all these reasons, plus the satisfaction of doing it yourself, it is very much worth while and a lot of fun to *Make Your Own Merry Christmas*.

It is a matter of universal experience that creative work of any kind increases and prolongs the enjoyment of the worker. We like the things we buy for a while, but we love the things we make for a long time. It seems to me that those who create something useful and beautiful in honor of Christmas, with their own hands and hearts and imaginations, will live in the true spirit of Christmas long after the tree comes down. If they do, in some degree they make this world a better place.

Many friends have encouraged and inspired me to write this little book. I am in debt to them all, and to the many patient audiences which have listened to lectures on the subject. Actually, I have practiced on these kind people, for the suggestions made in this book have been accumulating for many years and it is still possible to find new ways and means of making your own Merry Christmas. By talking and demonstrating before so many critical audiences, moreover, I believe I have worked out practical methods of making these decorations, within the ability of anybody willing to spend a little time and effort in mastering them.

Another debt of repentant acknowledgment is due my family whose interest and tolerance have been remarkable, considering how often and completely I have cluttered the house with my hobby.

My deep gratitude goes also to Helen Van Pelt Wilson, who overcame my natural reluctance for writing and persuaded me to put the substance of my lectures within covers. Also to Dr. J. Horace McFarland, for his kind introduction. And to The Pennsylvania Horticultural Society for the use of its offices and library.

To name all the helpful individuals would be impossible, but I offer special thanks to Henry S. Ross and Don Rose for editorial advice and assistance; to Harry Wood for his help with plant materials used in many demonstrations; to my family and friends who kindly gave me favorite recipes and finally and particularly to Léonie Hagerty for the clever drawings which largely take the place of my own fingers in this book. It would be difficult to explain some of the procedures with words alone. Miss Hagerty's diagrams and sketches confirm a paraphrased Chinese proverb, "One look-see is worth a million tells."

ANNE WERTSNER

Germantown, Philadelphia

Contents

1 . . . Looking Forward to Christmas

CHRISTMAS COMES but once a year, but its enjoyment need not be limited to a few crowded days in December. Anything so nice as Christmas deserves to be anticipated a long time in advance and remembered a long time afterwards. This is true of many pleasures. Much of the fun of a trip is found in planning it, deciding where to go, what to see, what to wear, how much to spend. So why not spread the fun of this festival through the year, by planning and preparing for it in every season?

A good time to look forward to Christmas is when you have just finished enjoying one. Then you may be full of ideas for next year. And if you plan to make your own decorations, there will be added delight in finding and storing the materials you will need—and in getting them as cheaply as possible.

A shopping spree right after Christmas may disclose some exciting bargains. Many expensive decorations are sold at half price or less, because it would require too much space to store them for another season. A small closet shelf would hold them easily, together with tree ornaments and lights, and it will be like finding treasure-trove to discover them there next December.

On the same shelf might be kept a special Christmas notebook. It would contain addresses of stores that carry the things needed to make a Merry Christmas. Certain stores specialize in candles. It is convenient to know where they are when candles are wanted. There are out-of-the-way gift shops which can supply unusual candle holders in various sizes and designs. Make a note of them; then buy the holders when your plans for Christmas decorating are complete.

It may even be a good idea to do a little housecleaning when Christmas is over. Why keep damaged decorations for another year? Tree ornaments in poor colors or silly shapes might as well be discarded at once.

Summer can be a productive season for the farsighted planner. Vacation trips may take us to places where cones, seed pods, bark, twigs and other materials can be had for the taking. Sources of useful materials, such as evergreens, berries, moss, wire and thread may be listed in the notebook. Some are difficult to get when everybody is buying in December. If they will store well, it is wise to acquire them when they are easily available.

There are adventures waiting for those who keep their eyes open, with Christmas in mind. While traveling in Texas a few years ago, I came across a beautiful white berry and brought some sprays back to Philadelphia. The berry is hard, pure white, and does not drop or shake off when dry. It resembles the familiar snowberry (Symphoricarpos albus), but has good qualities which the snowberry and bayberry lack. In Texas it is called Chinese tallow berry; in Charleston, South Carolina, the natives call it popcorn. The botanical name is Sapium sebiferum. It is the finest white berry I have ever found for Christmas decorations, and few northerners know about it or use it. I wouldn't know about it myself, probably, if I had not been thinking of Christmas in Philadelphia while traveling in Texas.

More familiar materials are plentiful in the early fall. Bayberry should be gathered then, the leaves removed, and branches tied in bunches and hung in an airy place to dry out thoroughly. Later on, in October or early November, branches of black alder berries (Ilex verticillata) may be cut and kept in water until needed. They will last much better than those bought in the shops, which have been in storage for some time.

Science has recently come to the aid of the decorator. By spraying with hormone preparations, many fruits and leaves or needles can be prevented from dropping. For those kept standing in water, it helps to add a complete fertilizer, one teaspoonful, or two or three tablets, per quart of water. The cut branches will continue to grow for some time and keep fresh for Christmas.

Obviously, not every attractive fruit or berry can be preserved for use some weeks or months later. A good guide is a pair of observant eyes; berries which stay on the bushes well into the winter can usually be kept fresh indoors for a long time. Examples are the red fruits of the multiflora rose, and the heavenly bamboo (Nandina domestica).

The mechanical aids of the decorator—wires of various weights, florists' thread, shellac and sharp shears—ought to be picked up and put away well in advance of their seasonal use. It will cost more money and take a lot of time to buy them when the shopping rush is on.

At any time of the year, next Christmas can be a thing of beauty in the mind's eye. It is a pleasant employment on a quiet evening to make plans, change them and make new ones. In the actual holiday excitement there may be no time for doing a really thoughtful and artistic job.

According to Emerson, an Indian once answered a white man who complained that he had no time, "You have all the time there is." The trouble is we don't always have it when we need it. The right time for planning is when there are not too many other things to do.

In out-of-season thinking, a few fundamentals should be kept in mind. It is important for decorations to harmonize with the house. Over-decoration is bad; it cheapens the total effect. A few well-made and carefully placed decorations will be far more attractive than a clutter of inferior ones.

Where there are wide windows, garlands may be appropriate across the tops. Large rooms may permit garlands around mantels or draped over banisters. But an evergreen ball suspended in a hall or doorway, or a candle board decoration on a window sill may be more effective in a small house.

Formal houses require a corresponding formality in treatment. The colors used are important. Too many people consider a confusion of colors appropriate for Christmas. Red and green and white are traditional, but there is no law on the subject. Modern taste approves blue and silver, or other combinations that suit the room and house in which they are used.

Size is important in respect to color. Too much heavy color in a small place may create a cramped and stuffy effect. Neither should small rooms be overloaded with evergreen boughs or wreaths or sprays. The ideal is good proportion.

It is an established custom in many homes to remove the Christmas decorations on a particular date. It is better to discard them while they are attractive than to become bored with them. There is nothing that looks more miserable than a tree which has outlasted its welcome, or a dried up wreath which has lost the life and sparkle which first gave it meaning.

2 . . . Making a Green Christmas

A WRITER of the seventeenth century declared that "a green Christmas is neither handsome nor healthful." He was referring to Christmas outdoors, of course. Indoors, the use of evergreens in decoration is traditional. It is interesting to note that evergreens were not used, at first, for their decorative value, but because of their symbolism.

In many parts of the world, any tree which seems to defy the killing cold of winter is given a mystical significance and is frequently associated with religious feasts and ceremonies. The evergreen tree serves this purpose beautifully. It brings nature indoors. The scent of some, such as the balsam fir, adds fragrance to beauty and builds up enduring memories. Perhaps the sense of smell is the most nostalgic of all. We are probably remembering our childhood when we say that a decorated room not only looks, but "smells like Christmas."

Americans inherited the use of evergreens for Christmas decorations from a varied ancestry. They have used them so freely and enthusiastically, indeed, that some species have been threatened by extinction. Fortunately, many people interested in conservation of our natural resources have paid due attention to the evergreens. They have made garden club members, if not others, aware of the fact that certain evergreens may be used freely, while others need protection from individuals carried away by Yuletide exuberance.

Each section of the United States has its own problem. Everywhere, or nearly everywhere, there is a wealth of plant material, but some species are plentiful in some states and scarce in others. For this reason conservation committees of garden clubs have published lists of plants that should not be used for decorations, or should be harvested carefully.

It is impossible to recommend plants for all sections. Everywhere, it seems to me, it is wise to use but not abuse, to cut carefully, and to plant and produce the evergreens most needed. In general it may be said that balsam fir, white pine, spruce, hemlock, red cedar, arborvitae, juniper, yew, box, ivy, barberry and privet are plentiful and may be used freely. Holly, laurel and ground pine are relatively scarce and should be used with respect and discretion.

Holly belongs to Christmas by tradition, but it does not flourish in the wild in all parts of the country. Fortunately for the Christmas decorator, it is now being grown commercially in many places, especially Oregon. There it is harvested properly and legally. This is also true of Christmas trees. Great numbers are sent to market from our national forests, where they are selected and cut with forethought for the future of our timberlands.

Sometimes scarcity is a good thing. It inspires a search for substitutes, and sometimes the substitute turns out to be more satisfactory than the original commodity. Because holly grew scarce and it was no longer quite respectable to use it freely for wreaths, decorators became interested in other appropriate greens. Now holly no longer commands the scene, for nearly every kind of plant supplies material for holiday decorations.

The center of the Christmas picture is still the tree itself. Many different trees may be used, but some are much better for the purpose than others. The best are the firs (Abies), the white, Nordmann and balsam, because they do not shed their needles. The balsam fir (Abies balsamea) has the added charm of fragrance. Many people do not know evergreens by name, but the difference between the fir and spruce can be detected by touch. Most firs are soft, while spruce trees are prickly as pincushions. More technically, fir needles are attached to their stems by suction-like cups at the base. In addition to the true firs, a tree of good qualities is the so-called Douglas fir (Pseudotsuga taxifolia).

Common hemlock is frequently used but would be much better left outdoors. As Emily Dickinson wrote, "the hemlock's nature thrives on cold," and its needles fall rapidly in the heat of the house, unless the tree or branches are kept in water. If the ends of hemlock stems are sharpened and inserted in white potatoes they will keep fairly fresh. This is true of all greens, but the hemlock properly belongs outdoors. The common hemlock (Tsuga canadensis) is a magnificent tree. Few can compare with it for grace and beauty. In winter, with its branches weighted down with snow, it is far more lovely than any man-made decorations of the season. And to walk in a grove of old hemlocks at any time of the year is a moving spiritual experience. The needles are a beautiful dark green, desirable and suitable for Christmas, but they drop so soon indoors that decorations in which they are used often grow shabby before they have been fully enjoyed.

Pines (Pinus) are not very popular for Christmas trees, though they are used in some parts of the country. The white pine and the Austrian are probably the most satisfactory. Red cedar (Juniperus virginiana) and arborvitae (Thuja) are seldom used, except in sections where they grow wild.

Many people like to trim living trees, which are certainly most attractive. Some gardeners can point with pride to trees that have celebrated a Merry Christmas and lived for many years more to add beauty to a home's surroundings. The spruces (Picea) are preferable for this purpose. The Norway spruce is least desirable, but also the least expensive in most localities. Indoors it is important to give living trees plenty of water so that they will not die soon after they are planted in the open.

So much for the choice and care of the tree. For wreaths and cut branches there is also a good selection of evergreens. Yew (Taxus) is a rich dark green, similar to hemlock, but more rigid. It does not shed its needles. Of the pines, the white, Scotch and yellow are the most popular. They are valuable for sprays and to work in among other evergreens of heavier texture and darker shades. They keep their needles well. The colors vary; one of the most useful is the white pine, a blue green which adds a light and airy look to other greens in wreaths and displays.

Arborvitae (Thuja), the junipers (Juniperus) and false-cypress (Chamaecyparis) may be had in many varieties. Chamaecyparis pisifera squarrosa is desirable for its color and feathery effect. There are other hues available in these greens—dark green, blue-green, yellowish or golden. The false cypress has the advantage of being easier to handle than the prickly spruces and junipers.

Many of the broad-leaved evergreens are suitable for our purpose. American holly (Ilex opaca) has dull leaves in contrast to the dark and shining foliage of the English holly (Ilex aquifolium). American holly is hardier than the English, but not nearly so handsome. The leaves and fruits of both are very decorative. The leaves of evergreens vary in size and color. Boxwood (Buxus), Japanese holly (Ilex crenata), western huckleberry (Vaccinium ovatum), and the evergreen barberries (Berberis) are all small-leaved. Rhododendrons, mountain laurel (Kalmia latifolia), evergreen privets (Ligustrum) and leucothoe have larger and longer leaves. Those of the galax are round, dark green and bronzy in color. English ivy (Hedera helix) also gives a rounded effect; the Oregon holly grape (Mahonia) and the hollies (Ilex) are more pointed.

Some plants should not be cut, unless they are plentiful on your own property. California laurel (Umbellularia californica), mountain laurel (Kalmia latifolia) and ground pine (Lycopodium) need protection until the supply increases. The lycopodiums spread by running stems, which careless harvesters root up in great masses. It takes seven years for a plant to reach maturity from a spore, so the need for protection is apparent.

All evergreens should be cut carefully with clean, sharp shears so that wounds will quickly heal. Proper cutting stimulates growth and thickens the plant. Although the correct time for pruning is before new growth starts, winter trimming does no harm.

Bundles of mixed evergreens are obtainable from most nurserymen at Christmas time. Many nurseries also ship gift boxes of greens, a present welcomed by those who make their own Merry Christmas. Collections usually include fir, leucothoe, galax leaves, holly and Scotch broom (Cytisus scoparius). The broom is linear in form and fine for arrangements. Add a few suitable berries to these gift materials, arrange them artistically, and a really satisfying decoration will result. (Drawing 23, top)

If these evergreens are not available in quantity, preparation for Christmas should not stop with buying and setting up a tree. Instead acquire two trees. Cut up the extra one for wreaths and other decorations.

3 . . . Fruit Out of Season

GREEN IS the background and foundation of the indoor Christmas, but the background may be brightened with all the colors of the rainbow. We may use many materials to accent decorations, but they should be selected with a sense of fitness. A colored candle may be suitable where a bright patch of fabric would be out of place.

Instinctively we turn to nature for color to enliven our displays. Nature is generous in supplying it. There is brilliance in fruits and berries, more subtle tones in cones and seed pods. All these are fruits, in fact, with different seasons. Only at Christmas time are they in season at the same time, if used ingeniously and artistically to beautify our homes.

Fruits present the problem of keeping them fresh and firm while they serve their purpose on a wreath or as a decorative accent. If sound fruit is handled carefully and thoroughly coated with shellac, it should last through the holidays in average temperatures. In extreme cold most fruits turn brown. At room temperature the fruit ripens, but may still keep quite well. As fruit matures and mellows its color usually changes, but forethought in its arrangement will allow for this alteration. For example, limes turn yellow as they ripen, while lemons, kumquats and lady apples turn brown. Cranberries shrivel, but stay red.

One fruit not very suitable for our purpose is the pear. Pears have a lot of flesh which ripens to softness. They are of awkward shape and difficult to work into a wreath; if desired, they are better for garlands or sprays.

The lady apple (Malus) a red fruit for decoration as well as the table, appears during the winter months. It should not be confused with the love apple (Solanum integrifolium) which is orange and inedible.

Grapes are suitable and offer varied rich colors. Artificial grapes will be easier to handle than fresh fruit. A coat of shellac makes them appear more natural.

The lesser fruits, which we call berries, are plentiful and usually available. There is enough variety among them to satisfy the most imaginative and original designer of decorations. Some of those suggested below can be purchased at florists' shops and nurseries; others can be found in fields and woods and gardens. It prolongs the enjoyment of Christmas to watch for them in our walks and travels and to plan ahead for their use.

With one notable exception, all berries may be coated with shellac to preserve them and heighten their colors. Shellac will spoil the dull gray surface of the beautiful bayberry. Nandina berries, if you can obtain some from the South, are true Christmas red and keep well. They do not shrivel or drop when dry. Deciduous holly or winterberry (Ilex verticillata) with berries similar to those of the common holly is probably the best that can be bought.

The fruit of the American holly (Ilex opaca) is a dull red in comparison to the shining scarlet of the English (Ilex Aquifolium). When these two are used, more fruit can be displayed by trimming out the leaves around them.

Fruits of the common barberry (Berberis thunbergi) are excellent in color, last well and withstand hard freezing. The barberry's thorniness makes it hard to handle, but beautiful effects can be created with its bright little berries.

Bittersweet (Celastrus scandens) is desirable and lasting in a color scheme calling for orange-yellow. Firethorn berries (Pyracantha) come in red, orange and yellow and keep fairly well, especially if the stem ends are placed in water. Rosa multiflora fruits grow in small red clusters and remain in good condition on the bush until Christmas.

Toyon or Christmas berry (Photinia arbutifolia) is widely used in the West. Its red berries combine beautifully with holly leaves. The fruits of ibota privet (Ligustrum ibota) are black with stems and berries which can be silvered or painted. The fruit stays on the stem well and withstands handling.

In my opinion the Chinese tallow berry (Sapium sebiferum) is the best of the white berries; it dries hard, does not shake off, handles easily and lasts indefinitely. Cotoneasters in variety may be had in some sections of the country. The fruits are a good red, some produced in showy clusters, others singly along the stem.

Small gourds ripening in many shapes and colors offer dramatic decorative effects. More delicate possibilities may be discovered in silvered and gilded pods of milkweed. The pods have a lovely sheen inside, which is a joy to those who seek subtle effects in their arrangements.

The fruit of most evergreens is the cone. Those unfamiliar with cones may not realize their value in creating distinctive decorations, but the subject is well worth a little study. They differ greatly in size, color and form. They may be produced in clusters, as on some of the spruces, or singly, as on the pines. The cone of the common hemlock is tiny, about half an inch long, but cones twenty inches long appear on Pinus Lambertiana.

The spruce bears nice cones, generally rather resinous. Resin may stain the decorator's hands, but is easily removed with alcohol. The cone of the red spruce (Picea rubens) is frequently used. The white pine (Pinus strobus) provides an attractive cone, its scales or segments tipped with a white resinous substance. When fresh, the white pine cone appears to have been dipped in snow. It is light in weight with scales far enough apart for easy wiring.

Some pine cones are difficult to handle. Their close-fitting scales remain tightly closed, even for years, and there are sharp, strong spines on the scales. The cones of pitch pine (Pinus rigida) and yellow pine (Pinus ponderosa) are popular. True cedar cones (Cedrus atlantica, C. Libani and C. Deodara) are very tight, solid masses. But they are interesting and individual, and their skillful use makes them conversation pieces among more conventional decorations. The small stems should be left on cones. Otherwise it will be necessary to drill them for wiring.

True firs have cones with scales close together. The Douglas, which is not a true fir, has light brown cones with loose scales and long bracts or appendages. The tallest trees in the world, the giant California redwoods (Sequoiadendron gigantea) have small cones about three or four inches long with scales opening only slightly.

Cones can be gathered in the forests at any time of year and it is an interesting hobby to collect them. The Christmas decorator will do so with a special purpose. This will make their varied shapes, sizes and colors of absorbing interest.

4 . . . Tools and Technique

As in most hobbies and handicrafts, the equipment for the making of a Merry Christmas may match the taste and pocketbook of the decorator. There are few essentials. There can be, if you please, a considerable variety of tools and quantities of materials on your Christmas shelf.

The essentials include a pair of sharp pruning shears, florists' thread, wire, shellac, white paint and small amounts of other colors, silver or aluminum and gilt paints, brushes, turpentine and plaster of Paris. Sphagnum moss is also useful.

Florists' thread is far better than thin string, which breaks when tightly pulled. This thread is made in several weights, but the amateur will find No. 6, which is somewhat like a strong, fast-colored green trout-fishing line, the most suitable.

Florists' wire, cut in 12- and 18-inch lengths, is useful in many ways. It is advisable to stock various thicknesses or weights of this wire. A good working supply would include some 18-inch lengths of No. 18, 12-inch lengths of No. 20 or No. 21 and of No. 25. The lower numbers represent the heavier wire. Some may find No. 18 hard to use at first, but a little experience will make it manageable. For most purposes I prefer stiffer wire. For frames, trees and wreaths I select No. 10 or even No. 9.

Shellac may be used for other purposes than preserving fruit. The variety of paints may be wide as you please, but I recommend the smallest can of each since only a little of any one color is needed. Plaster of Paris can be obtained in packages at any hardware or drug store. These are basic supplies. Complete equipment would also include Scotch tape, cellophane, cellophane glass sips, tin cans of various sizes, half-inch galvanized wire, a package of confetti, glitter (silver decorettes), glue, toothpicks, waterproof and satin ribbon.

For most decorations it will also be well to have on hand cones in various sizes, commercially prepared magnolia leaves, artificial holly berries and the berries of bayberry or other fruits which last well.

Aside from shears, the only tools to be used are a small pair of pliers and a drill for making holes through nuts or cones. But even these are not essential. Fingers were made before pliers, and a redhot hatpin will make neat holes through nuts or seed pods to prepare them for wiring.

Manpower may be needed for the construction of such items as bases for trees and candle boards. Any handy man can make these with common workshop tools and odds and ends of lumber. Women could do it, for that matter, but it is good strategy to give the menfolk a share in decorating for Christmas so that they will appreciate the final results.

Some people are baffled at first by wiring, but there is really no difficult trick to it. Wiring is necessary to hold fruits, cones and bows in position on wreaths and other decorations. With a little practice, wiring can be done neatly, firmly and inconspicuously. Any method is good which serves the purpose.

The weight of wire used depends on the weight of the material to be fastened. The No. 20 is strong enough to hold a white pine cone in place; heavier may be needed for the cone of the Douglas fir. Length of wire will depend on size of cone, 12- or 18-inch pieces usually suffice.

Cones are wired by wedging one end of the wire under a few lower segments, then turning it several times around the base, among the segments, until the cone is firmly attached. Even tight cones can be fastened in this way, though it is easier to wire these if a little of the stem is left on each one. When the cone is attached to the wire, there should be about eight inches of wire remaining for insertion into the greens and winding around the frame on which they are to be arranged. (Drawings 1 and 7)

In all wiring, allow for the fact that greens and the stems of plants shrink as they dry. This calls for firm work. The placing of the cones, when wired, is determined by their type. Some cones, like those of Scotch and yellow pine, may be wired and fastened upside down to the frame. This treatment gives a flat, solid appearance. A rose-like effect can be attained by cutting crosswise through large cones, then using the halves.

Bayberry, English holly and nandina may come in bunches big enough to use as individual sprays. Other berries need to be wired together for a bunched effect. A strand of No. 18 or No. 19 wire is twisted several times around the grouped stems before they are fastened where the decorator pleases. (Drawing 1)

Fruits are usually laid horizontally on the decoration, and are easy to wire in this position. The wire, an 18-inch length of No. 18, is thrust through the fruit and twisted securely behind it. (Drawing 4)

A different technique is used with grapes and cranberries. The stem end of a bunch of grapes is fastened to the frame with a 12-inch length of wire. Then close to the end of the bunch of grapes another wire, hairpin-shaped, is placed over the stem and twisted firmly to the frame. Cranberries are more troublesome. They look unnatural if wired. Yet properly used they add as much to a wreath as a sprinkling of Jordan almonds to a box of chocolates. The solution is to impale cranberries on

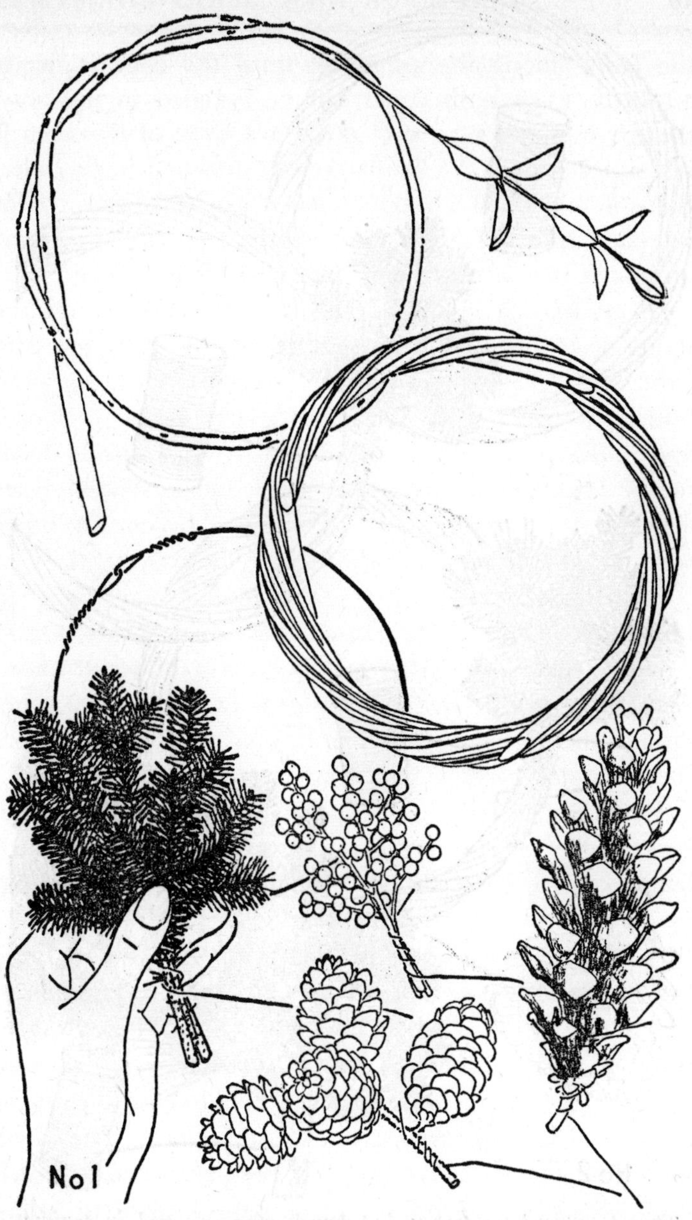

Twisted privet cane; completed privet frame for heavy green wreath; wire hoop for light weight wreath; wired berries, cones and greens.

Thread fastened on frame; first bunch of greens tied in position; thread drawn tightly between stems and frame to keep from slipping, one continuous piece carried around until end; lastly, decorations are wired in position.

Looping of ribbon for bow, one end covers the wire twisted around center; wire holds end of ribbon in position; bow fastened to wreath with wire.

toothpicks and then to wire them in bunches of three to the decoration. (Drawing 4)

It is necessary to bore holes in most nuts, acorns, some eucalyptus pods, sycamore balls, and the fruit of the sweet gum, in order to wire them. As with fruits, the wire ends should be twisted in back of the nut, where they will not show on the finished decoration. It may be easier to girdle a walnut. (Drawing 7)

The wires will show on the back of the wreath or spray, of course, but they should not stick out. It is a simple matter to turn the ends into the greens, and avoid annoying scratches and pinpricks for those who handle the decorations. Loose ends of wire may also scratch doors, or get caught in table coverings. A workmanlike job of wiring makes a neat decoration, easily handled, and unlikely to fall apart or lose shape and pattern. It really requires only a little practice to master wiring, though it may sound somewhat complicated.

After wiring, the next mechanical process is that of shellacking. A coat of white shellac gives a nice gloss, prevents loss of moisture, fills holes made by the wire and also seems to arrest the process of decay in fruits and berries. The best method is to shellac each piece after it is wired, using a small brush and protecting the worktable with sheets of newspaper. Some may prefer a sprayer, but this is more troublesome to clean than a brush. Dipping fruit, berry or cone into shellac is less desirable; it requires more shellac and the thicker resulting coat takes longer to dry and dulls the colors.

Bows of ribbon, made by looping, are given two twists of wire around the center, with enough wire to spare for fastening to wreath or spray. Sometimes the ribbon is drawn over the wire to conceal it. (Drawing 3)

Cellophane straws or glass sips are prepared for use by twisting a 12-inch length of wire around the middle of a bunch of them. When the wire is pulled tight the straws spread out from the center.

Pompons, which are pleasing in many decorative pieces, may be made of cellophane, using strips about 10 inches wide and 18 inches long. The cellophane is gathered through the center, along the length, and twisted around the center with a 12-inch wire. (Drawing 19) Tight twisting, as with the straws, forces the cellophane forward into pompon shape. Leave both ends of the wire protruding, like a hairpin, so that the pompons can be fastened in place.

5 . . . *Trimming the Tree*

THERE ARE universal traditions of Christmas and customs that are generally honored. There are others, no less important, that have grown up through the years in individual homes and families. These traditions and customs may determine when the tree is to be set up and decorated, who is to do it, and how it is to be done. The suggestions in this chapter are made in the hope of increasing these joyous time-honored, family traditions.

The more technical details of selecting a Christmas tree were discussed in Chapter 2. It may be added here that the tree should be chosen with some regard for the size of the room which it is to adorn. I have seen oversized trees with their tops taken off standing in low-ceilinged rooms like sliding poles in a city firehouse. A small tree may look better on a low table than on the floor. A thin or badly proportioned tree can be much improved by wiring extra branches into the bad spots.

In my opinion, nothing has ever surpassed the beauty of the traditional Christmas tree, sparkling with old-fashioned balls and ornaments, for the most part imported from countries where their making was an ancient art. Perhaps there are many people who have never seen what I call a traditional tree. This may be why so many substitutes for the old-fashioned ornaments have come into use—paper rings, small toys, rope tinsel, fruits, icicles and fancy lights. There is no law against using any of these, but when the effect is shoddy, as it so often is, I find myself with a feeling of nostalgia wishing for a tree with ornaments bright and beautiful and a total effect simple and really artistic.

Some people regret that candles no longer decorate trees. They were a serious fire hazard, of course, but their flickering lights and even the smoke and smell of the candles seemed appropriate to Christmas. When trees are trimmed with balls and ornaments, the smaller should be at the top with an imperceptible gradation toward the larger ones at the bottom. This gives an impression of stability and balance.

Color arrangement is a matter of taste. Some people prefer a single color, usually red, or a combination of blue and silver. I prefer the multi-colored tree. One color can be tiresome, or may quarrel with some outstanding furnishing. A proper tree *belongs* in the room at Christmas time. It does not stand there like a stranger.

Trees may be sprayed with aluminum paint for a silvered effect or with water or casein paints. A solid color requires two coats. Painted trees are hardly appropriate to Christmas in the home, though they may be striking in long rows in a hotel lobby or town hall. Special occasions may excuse the painting of a Christmas tree. I have seen, for example, an effective tree set up in honor of a new baby. It was given two coats of white casein paint, then decorated with strings of pink popcorn, booties, rattles and other delicate-colored gifts, tied on with light blue ribbon.

Electric lights add life and additional color to the tree, but often the passers-by on the street get a better view of them than the family indoors. It calls for a little ingenuity to hide the necessary wires and make the lights stand as upright as the candles they replace. Twelve-inch lengths of wire are helpful in this respect. Electric lights are suitable for outdoor trees. In choosing colors, consider that some carry better than others. White has higher visibility than amber; amber is brighter than red. Green or blue have a relatively short range. White bulbs with colored reflectors are effective.

It is a matter of good judgment, it seems to me, to avoid using traffic colors on an outdoor tree if it stands close to the street. Motorists find the multiplication of red and green lights confusing at Christmas time, especially when they are on community trees at crossroad locations.

True tinsel has not been available for some time. It tarnishes quickly and new materials have replaced it, but they do not have the fineness and sparkle of the old-fashioned kind. Thin strips of tinfoil are much used nowadays in place of tinsel. These should be hung lightly at the top of tree and a little thicker at the bottom.

Imitation snow, in some form, is attractive on the Christmas tree. Absorbent cotton is commonly employed for the purpose, but rock wool is better. Commercially prepared snow, which is really mica, adds sparkle and camphor flakes are a fairly good substitute. The easiest snow for home use is made by beating a cup of soap flakes into a half cup of water. Work it to the consistency of stiff-beaten white of egg. Then swish it onto the tree with a flip of the hand. It hardens quickly and stays pure white. It is equally effective when sprinkled on the twiggy branches of deciduous trees and on shrubs like hackberry and huckleberry used in other decorations around the house.

After the Christmas tree has served its purpose, it is usually discarded with scant ceremony. There is nothing quite so sad and sorry-looking as a bedraggled tree, draped with disheveled tinsel, waiting on the curb to be taken to the city dump. This is a tragic ending for a noble tree that was a short time ago the center of life and gaiety.

Some more dignified obsequies may be suggested. In small communities the trees might be taken to a vacant lot or hilltop, where there is no danger of fire spreading, and burned with ceremony and the singing of carols. Twelfth Night would be a good time for it, and some communities have done this. To add beauty to the fire, chemicals can be tossed in which will produce colorful flames. (See Chapter 10)

A practical use for the Christmas trees and greens is to cut them up to mulch flower beds or evergreens, as protection against the winter cold and the sun and the wind of spring. If this is done, tinsel should be removed. It is not appropriate in the garden. A large tree might be placed outdoors as a feeding station for the birds. Suet tied to the branches will attract woodpeckers, nuthatches and chickadees.

For use in public places, Christmas trees are treated to make them fire-resistant. It is impossible to make a tree absolutely fireproof, but proper treatment will make it unlikely that it will catch fire from any ordinary cause, such as a spark from the fireplace or a fault in the wiring of lights. A dry tree, of course, is inflammable if it has not been treated. This is why all trees and greens displayed in military hospitals must be fireproofed.

It takes a little time and effort to treat a tree, but it is certainly worth the trouble in households where there are small children. Some trees burn more readily than others. A freshly cut tree, of course, will not burn as quickly as one partially dried out. A simple precaution is to keep the tree as fresh as possible. When it is taken home, a small portion can be cut from the trunk and the tree placed in water. If left outdoors it may freeze, but this will keep it fresh until it is needed indoors.

Treatment for fire-resistance should be done several days before the tree is brought indoors. There are several methods. The most thorough is to use ammonium phosphate, enough to equal one-quarter the weight of the tree. Dissolve the chemical at the rate of one pound to one and a half pints of water. Make a fresh cut at the base of the tree and stand it in the solution, in a cool room, until the liquid has been absorbed. Ordinarily this will take from three to four days.

Another method is to spray the tree or cut branches of evergreens thoroughly with a similar solution, using one pound of ammonium phosphate to ten gallons of water. Half a gallon will coat a six- to eight-foot tree. The treatment leaves little residue and is in no way objectionable. Spraying should be done outdoors and the tree and greens allowed to dry before they are taken inside. Bows, ornaments and fruits should not be attached until after the spraying. It is advisable to spread newspapers on the area where the work is done; they will absorb excess liquid and prevent discoloration of the work surface.

Trees are considerably less of a fire hazard if they are securely fastened in their stands, so that they cannot topple toward a fireplace or candle flame. The danger of fire is further lessened by using a stand that holds water. An ordinary bucket will serve the purpose. Place the trunk in the bucket; then surround it with stones or gravel to the top. A wooden wedge, driven down into the ballast around the trunk, makes the tree more secure. Add water to the contents of the bucket and keep it filled through the holidays.

A cut tree will last longer if supplied with plant food. Use any complete chemical fertilizer at the rate of one teaspoonful to a quart of water. The nutrient solution, absorbed by the tree, will stimulate temporary growth which will keep the tree green and fresh for a week or so. About a quarter pound of complete fertilizer will be required for the first filling of the bucket; it may be mixed with water in advance or put on the stones or gravel before water is added.

These simple precautions add much to the enjoyment of Christmas by minimizing the danger of fire, which sometimes turns a happy holiday into tragic disaster.

6 . . . *The Making of Wreaths*

FOR SOME PEOPLE it is a commonplace chore of Christmas to buy a wreath or two, usually at a fancy price, and hang the purchase on the front door or above the fireplace. Yet a really handsome wreath can be made for a nominal sum and the satisfaction of designing and making it will add tremendously to its enjoyment. New ideas for making wreaths will come with every Christmas.

The equipment needed is shears, thread and wire. The mechanics can be mastered with a little practice. The foundation or frame is important; on a bad frame it is almost impossible to make a good wreath.

Drawing 1 shows how a frame may be constructed from switches of willow or any pliable shrub. The best canes for the purpose are those of ordinary California privet (Ligustrum ovalifolium). Privet may be bent into any size hoop without splitting or breaking. For an average wreath you will need canes four or more feet long, and as thick as your little finger. These should be stripped of leaves and side branches. If they are cut in very cold weather, it may be necessary to bend the canes back and forth until they are flexible.

Hold the cane at its thick end. Then make the size circle desired. Next twist the thin end in, over and out of the circle until it is completely used. One long cane may be sufficient; two or more make a stronger frame. Whether to use one or more canes depends on the size of the wreath, the thickness of the canes and the materials with which the wreath is to be decorated. Heavy fruits call for a stronger frame than cones or leaves.

If a second cane is to be added to the ring, place the thick end of it on the ring at a point beyond the entry of the first cane, or else work the second cane into the thinnest part of the hoop. Twist it in the same direction as the first cane. Trim off the stubs of the canes with shears, so that no ends stick out from the circle. The hoops will need no tying, but are now ready for use, as shown in Drawing 1.

I prefer these privet frames to those made of wire. The thread with which the greens are tied does not slip on the canes as it tends to on wire.

Wire frames may be purchased, if raw materials for making your frames are not available. A wire circle can be formed by rounding out an ordinary metal coat hanger. More ambitious craftsmen make wire frames from 8-foot lengths of No. 14 iron wire; the result is a hoop 10 to 12 inches in diameter. This wire is not too hard to handle without tools. A heavier wire, perhaps No. 9, makes a sturdy single-circle hoop if the ends are neatly hooked together. This will require pliers. (Drawing 1)

Sometimes frames are packed with moss, into which the stems of evergreens are inserted or evergreens may be wired to toothpicks and thrust into the moss. I find this type of frame cumbersome and not suitable for hanging on a door. If you do use one, take care that the colored paper wrapped around the moss does not rub off on the door or other background, as it may if the moss is damp.

When frames are ready, evergreens should be cut and prepared. It requires about four pounds of greens to fashion an average wreath. Mixed greens are recommended. It is easier to make a good circle with varied materials, and more effective too. Another advantage is that if some materials dry out there will remain enough green and fresh ones. A good combination consists of arborvitae, fir, cedar and white pine. Any broadleaf evergreen, not too large, can be worked in. The broad-leaved evergreens are excellent for displaying the beauty of fruits in a wreath.

A coat of white shellac prevents the shriveling of greens. Shellac may be applied with brush or spray, and first to the under side of the leaf. A coat on the stem holds moisture in and helps keep leaves fresh.

The beginner will be wise to prepare evergreens in advance of actual fastening to the frame, grouping them in bunches convenient for handling. The bunches should be six inches or more in length, depending on the size of the hoop. Every third bunch on the frame may include a piece of broadleaf evergreen, such as leucothoe, box, ivy or galax.

Thin wire may be used to bind the greens to the frame, but I prefer fast-colored florists' thread, No. 6. First fasten the binding thread or wire securely to the frame. Tie on a bunch of greens by pulling the binder tightly around the lower two inches. Four or five turns are sufficient. (Drawing 2) The wrapping should cover at least an inch of the stem, or the bunch will not remain in place on the frame. The binder is carried around the frame in one continuous piece and is not cut until the wreath is completed. If it is necessary to leave the work before it is finished, the wire or thread may be anchored by pulling it between the frame and the stem ends of the greens. (Drawing 2)

The bunches of greens need not be large or thick. If too much material is put into them, the wreath will be too heavy. Enough should be used so that you cannot see through the wreath, but no more.

The second bunch should overlap the stems of the first. With a little care it is easy to make a continuous line. The size of the final wreath is partly determined by the arrangement of the bunches; if they are set at an angle, the wreath will be larger than if they follow the contour of the frame.

Making a good joint between the last bunch of greens and the first requires care. Here the thread is cut and knotted. This finishing is more easily accomplished if the wreath is turned over.

Beginners tend to pull the greens in the direction in which the binder is pulled. This can be prevented by carrying the thread or wire from inside the center of the hoop out over the top. Work the greens in counter-clockwise. (Drawing 2) The pulling is then toward you and makes for tighter wreaths, less likely to fall apart as they dry. This also insures a hole in the center of the wreath. If the thread is drawn toward the center, the greens may become a solid mass.

When they are all attached, the wreath is ready for decoration. It is advisable first, however, to hold it to the light or before a mirror to check for weak spots. Defects can often be detected in this way.

If the wreath appears heavier or larger in one section, this should be chosen for the bottom of the finished decoration. Small white pine cones can be wired in to fill gaps or round out the circle.

Decoration of the wreath may be simple or elaborate. Fruits or nuts may be used. Good effects are possible with cellophane, candy canes, Christmas tree ornaments, magnolia leaves, ivy, herbs, bunches of artificial grapes and many other materials. (Drawing 6) Perhaps the most elaborate wreath is the Della Robbia which is decorated with shellacked fruits to resemble the ornamental borders of glazed and colored terra cotta which Luca Della Robbia and his family made in the fifteenth century. He was an outstanding artist of the Renaissance and his craftsmanship is familiar to all artists and travelers. (Drawing 4)

For this striking wreath a variety of fruits may be

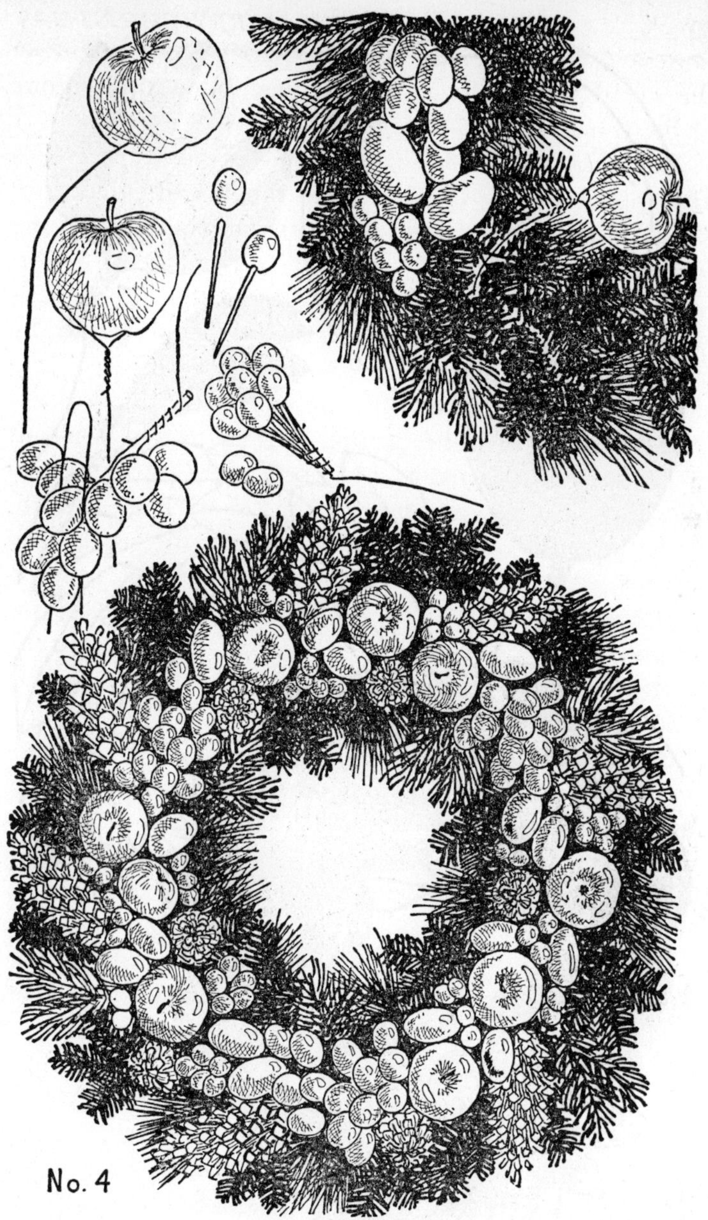

Fresh fruits of lady apples, kumquats, limes, lemons, wired and fastened to wreath. Cranberries impaled on toothpicks are wired in small bunches. Hairpin shaped piece of wire holds end of bunch of grapes in position.

Double wire frame is used for light weight magnolia wreath. Groups of three leaves are wired flat or folded in half. Leaves may be wired in same direction or from top down.

Wreath of magnolia leaves wired flat. Artificial glass fruit is separate wreath. Both on wire frames are fastened together. Artificial glass bunches of grapes are fastened to wire frame to form lower wreath.

used: lady apples, limes, lemons, kumquats, grapes, cranberries and cones. Each piece is wired on separately. (See Chapter 4) The cranberries round out the border and accent it with their dark red color. This type of wreath may be used on the door, in a hallway, against paneling or as a centerpiece. As a centerpiece it may be placed on a mirror to add height to the table. Tall red candles may be placed at either end. Use fairly thick ones; thin candles will not balance the weight of the wreath unless several are used.

A simpler wreath may be made of mixed greens, decorated with cones, bayberry and red berries. If berries are scarce, a few red lady apples will provide color. A red bow looks well on this kind of wreath. Satin ribbon is effective if the wreath is to hang under cover, but waterproof fabric is necessary for an outdoor display. Oilcloth is waterproof, but is a poor substitute for ribbon. It makes a stiff and unnatural bow and looks exactly like what it is—oilcloth! (Drawing 3)

Artificial fruit with remarkable resemblance to the real article may occasionally be found in stores. Some people object to artificial material, but I see nothing wrong with it if shapes and colors are true. After all, it is the form and coloring, not the flavor, which is important in creating decorations. Artificial fruits can be wired to the frames in the same way as the real product. If it is in bunches, these can be cut apart and the individual pieces placed according to the decorator's discretion. A striking effect can be secured by making on separate frames one wreath of fruit and another of magnolia leaves and then wiring them together. (Drawing 6, top)

Magnolia leaves, commercially prepared and supplied by florists, are a reddish brown in color, easy to work with when damp, though very brittle when dry. The amateur can prepare leaves that will last for one season, though not indefinitely, as the commercial ones do. The leaves of the swamp magnolia (Magnolia glauca) are gathered when they turn brown and drop, and are then dipped in melted paraffin and ironed between sheets of newspaper.

For a flat wreath leaves are wired in threes, spread out like a fan. (Drawing 5, center) A 12-inch piece of No. 20 wire is inserted through the lower ends of the leaves and twisted around the stems several times. The remainder of the wire suffices to fasten them to the frame. The three leaves should be overlapped or assembled in the same pattern in each group so that the wreath will be uniform all around.

An effective magnolia wreath is made by starting in opposite directions on the frame and working groups of leaves down each side. Decoration is used only at the bottom, where the stem ends meet. The junction may be rounded out with smaller leaves. A little gilt paint on the tips of the lowest leaves gives a pleasing effect. Gilded acorns, love apples, bittersweet or artificial fruits may be similarly applied. Kumquats are suitable in size and color. (Drawing 5)

A permanent wreath may be stored safely if it is dusted, wrapped in waxed paper and packed in a box. If a change is desired when Christmas comes around again, the gilt can be painted over with aluminum paint. Sprays of bayberry may be used in place of the fruits. Illustrations of magnolia wreaths appear in Drawing 5. In these, the leaves were wired in groups of three. Then each leaf was folded forward in half. A 12-inch length of wire was inserted through the base of the leaves and around the stems as shown at top of Drawing 5.

The nut wreath takes the most time to make, but the result is worth it. My original one made over ten years ago is still my favorite. For the first year of storing it was

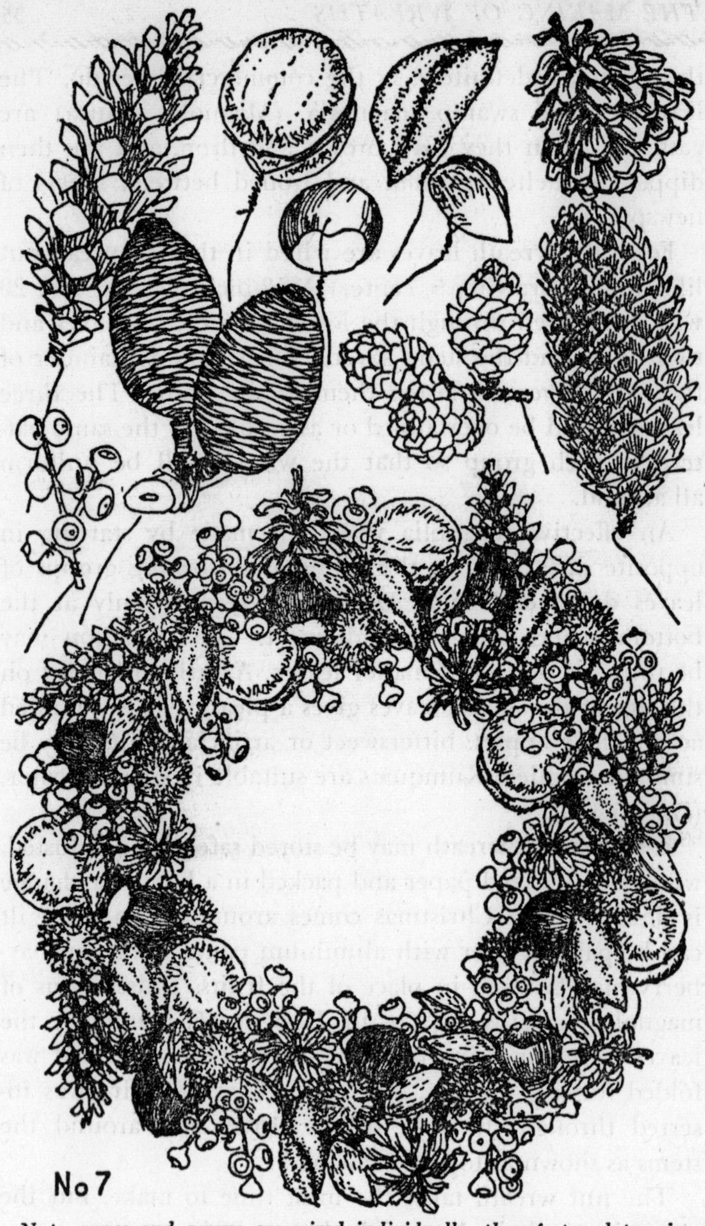

Nuts, cones and acorns are wired individually, then fastened to wire frame to make permanent nut wreath.

necessary to put dichloride crystals in the box, in order to prevent weevils. Now the nuts are thoroughly dry and the wreath keeps as well from season to season as an artificial one.

There is great variety possible in the making of nut wreaths. Acorns, Brazil nuts, chestnuts, litchi nuts, almonds, buttonball seed pods, sweet gum fruits, cones and bayberry provide a wide choice of forms and colors (Drawing 7) Sometimes unity gives a better effect than variety. A very handsome wreath can be made of small cones in different sizes some face up and others in reverse, either in natural colors or gilded.

Many of the sweet herbs may be used in wreaths, among them rosemary, gray artemisias, lavender, mullein and santolina. Some add the charm of a subtle fragrance.

A wreath of English holly with full berry clusters would need no other decoration, unless it were a red bow. And nothing else is required if a wreath is constructed mainly of dark-colored greens, with pieces of golden arborvitae, blue spruce or gray-foliaged plants worked in for occasional accents or contrast.

Simple, but quite effective, is a wreath of blue spruce, decorated with the brown buds (not the seed pods) of the Chinese empress tree (Paulownia tomentosa). Variegated holly and osmanthus leaves, decorated with limes and lemons, produce a beautiful and unusual effect in yellow-green. A more striking combination results when the flat silvery-white seed cases of honesty (Lunaria annua) are fashioned into a wreath and hung against red velvet. Other dramatic possibilities will occur to the imaginative and ingenious decorator. A wreath of golden arborvitae, with an inside circle of gilded ivy leaves, may serve as frame for a round picture of the Madonna, to be hung against old gold brocade.

After conventional forms and materials become familiar, there is opportunity for experiment. It is exciting to discover, for example, what can be done with mahonia leaves and white grapes, or with shellacked ivy leaves and tiny white onions. Possible diversities of color and effect are astonishing and unlimited. Anyone with a keen eye and an alert imagination may create a wreath of outstanding beauty from roadside materials. Every meadow and hedgerow has something of beauty and use to offer. The more commonplace the material, the greater the satisfaction in using it in distinctive and effective fashion.

7 . . . Hanging Decorations

THE CHRISTMAS TREE is usually the highlight of the home during the festive season. Other focal points are the front door, the fireplace and perhaps a hall. Window frames, open stairways, the mantelpiece and openings between rooms may also be adorned.

Good decoration consists of much more than sticking a few branches of evergreens behind curtain rods or pictures. Well-made garlands, sprays and hanging decorations can be suitably designed for each room and its furnishings. Fortunately, it is comparatively easy to make them.

The spray, sometimes called a swag, is simpler in construction than a wreath and requires less material. It may be used in any place where a wreath would be appropriate and is particularly attractive for brightening a mantel, a newel post or a narrow space between windows.

A few branches of pine neatly wired together may be the basis for a beautiful spray. Various decorations may be added. One large cone may be sufficient, or several small cones may be bunched to simulate a large one. A red bow completes a spray requiring little time or money, yet it is handsome as many an expensive commercial product. (Drawing 8)

When grouping branches for the spray, start with the largest. Then add the lesser branches. The main branch should not be too broad, or the spray will be out of proportion when completed. Stem ends should be cut obliquely, with the cut surface toward the back of the spray. This is a minor detail, but makes considerable difference in the final effect, which should include no

No 8

A large cone wired on long needle pine is effective with satin bow. Flower pots against spruce, fir or pine are unique; sleigh bells, cones and greens make attractive door pieces.

glaring white cuts. Some of the greens may be turned upward and wired inconspicuously to cover stems. These are further concealed by the attached cones and the bow. The bow is wired on when all other work is finished.

There is ample opportunity for variety in swags. A few sleigh bells worked into a door spray will jingle a welcome to every visitor. (Drawing 8) If you are fortunate enough to own a set of bells, or a long strip of bell harness, arrange it as a base for a spray or garland of evergreens. Berries and cones, of course, may be worked into any such arrangement.

Convincing artificial snowballs and icicles can be made by soaking newspaper and rolling or squeezing it into the desired shape. A string is tied to the ball or icicle which is then coated with a thin mixture of plaster of Paris prepared by adding warm water and stirring rapidly. The plaster hardens in a few minutes.

The decorator who is also a gardener may bring a summer hobby into the Christmas scene by using new clay flowerpots in various small sizes, hung upside down, as bells on sprays or wreaths. One design uses a branch as crosspiece from which pots are suspended by knotted cords. From the knot, inside the pot, a round bell may be hung as a clapper. It is wise to place flowerpots against a background of fir or other soft evergreen to prevent scratching of woodwork. (Drawing 8)

Crossed candy canes are an amusing touch, and one to delight children. They can be used on doors, grilles or fences outdoors, or indoors in place of wreaths or sprays. Wooden canes are selected in sizes proportionate to the place they are to decorate. They may be painted with quick-drying white enamel and wound with red waterproof ribbon tacked or fastened with Scotch tape. For small canes choose red Scotch tape, which comes in widths up to half an inch. Two crossed canes, tied with bright

The flat tree, useful for a doorpiece, is made on ½ inch mesh galvanized wire by inserting small pieces of evergreen. Cranberries and red yarn give color. Crossed red and white canes brighten a grille.

red ribbon, are effective against a dark background. Greens may be added. (Drawing 9)

A simulated Christmas tree on the front door offers a pleasant greeting to every caller. To make it, cut a piece of half-inch galvanized wire to the desired size and shape. Insert small pieces of spruce or fir through the mesh of the wire; the needles will catch and hold the pieces in place. Attach the greens in the way that shingles are put on a roof, starting with the bottom row and overlapping each succeeding row. Decorate with single cranberries or with pieces of popcorn wired into position. Red yarn makes a striking outline for the base. (Drawing 9)

A similar flat tree for the wall of a large room, a public hall or church, may be constructed with chicken wire cut to size and shape. Greens are tied on with hairpin-shaped pieces of wire. Gift tables, small tableaux, Christmas villages and even old Santa Claus himself will look well against such a background.

Other door pieces may be constructed on coat hangers. The crosspiece of the wire hanger is bent toward the top to increase the slope of the sides. The next step is to hold branches of evergreens on each side and place a piece to cover the top. A wire twisted around the neck of the hanger keeps them from slipping. A few whitened branches may be added, some berries wired in and a bow placed in the center. If all materials are at hand, this piece takes only a few minutes. (Drawing 10)

Garlands are made in the same way as wreaths. Greens are tied or wired to a rope or some other pliable material, instead of to a frame, so that the garland may be gracefully draped where it is wanted. It is well to cut the rope to size in advance. Cuting when finished will loosen the whole piece.

If the garland is to decorate a mantel and hang down on each side, it is preferable to make it in two sections and

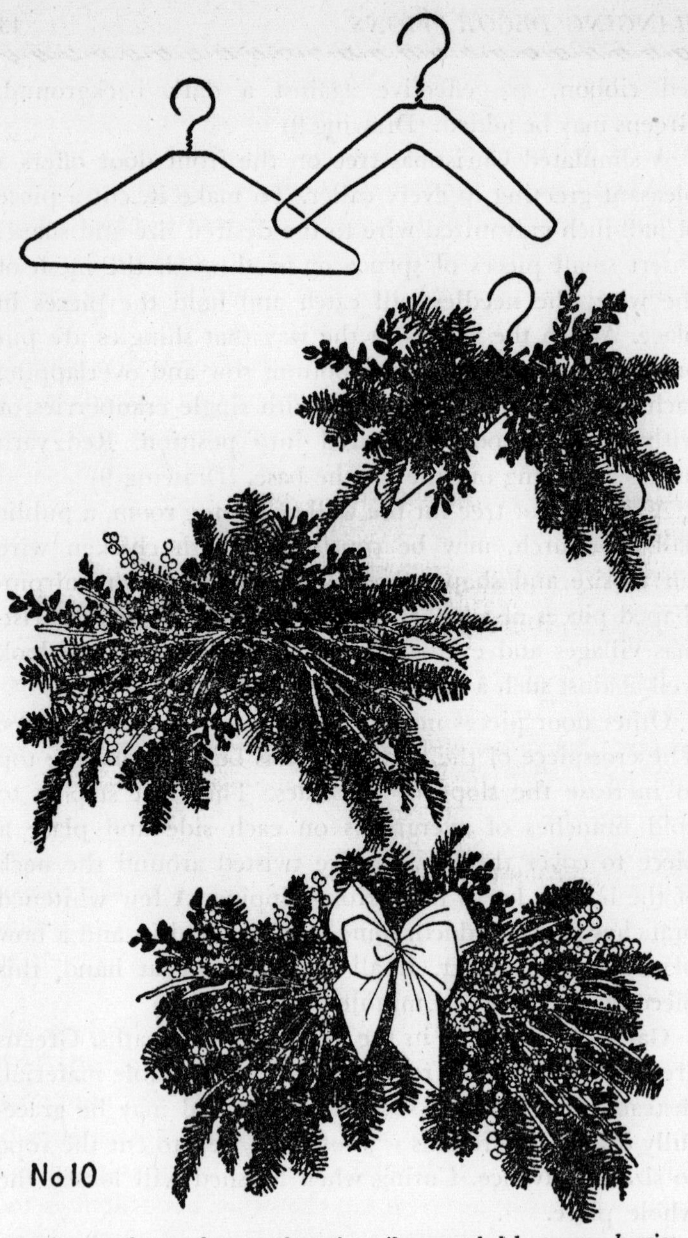

A wire coat hanger bent to shape is easily concealed by greens, berries, whitened branches, cones and a bow wired into position. It is a quick easy-to-make piece.

join them at the center. Otherwise greens hang down on one side and face up on the other. The joint may be easily hidden by greens or decorations. (Drawing 11)

When making a garland, fasten the rope at one end to a nail or doorknob or to something else stationary to keep it taut during the binding. Cover the rope with pieces or bunches of evergreen, about four inches long. Do not use too much or the result will be clumsy.

Any greens which do not drop as they dry may be selected. When coniferous evergreens are chosen, a few pieces of the broadleaved evergreens may be shellacked and placed in back of the garland, as is done with wreaths. If garlands are to be hung against brown paneling or woodwork, a rich effect may be attained with golden arborvitae decorated with limes, lemons, avocado pears and grapefruit. For a contrasting touch of white, add small onions.

Nearly all decorations made much in advance of Christmas should be kept outdoors or in a damp, cold place inside. Then they will keep well for two weeks or more and be perfectly fresh when hung indoors. If there is snow on the ground, the greens may be buried in it. If sprinkled with water they may freeze in bitter weather, but no harm will be done. The exception to the rule is that greens or trees treated to make them fire-resistant must be kept dry. In the case of garlands it is well to work before the Christmas rush begins.

An attractive decoration for hanging in a hallway, on the porch or in a bay window is the evergreen ball. This is made by shaping a generous handful of sphagnum moss into a ball and tying it all around with florists' thread. The moss must not be too hard or the ends of greens cannot be easily inserted. On the other hand, if it is too loose, they will fall out. (Drawing 11)

The stem ends of greens to be used should be stripped

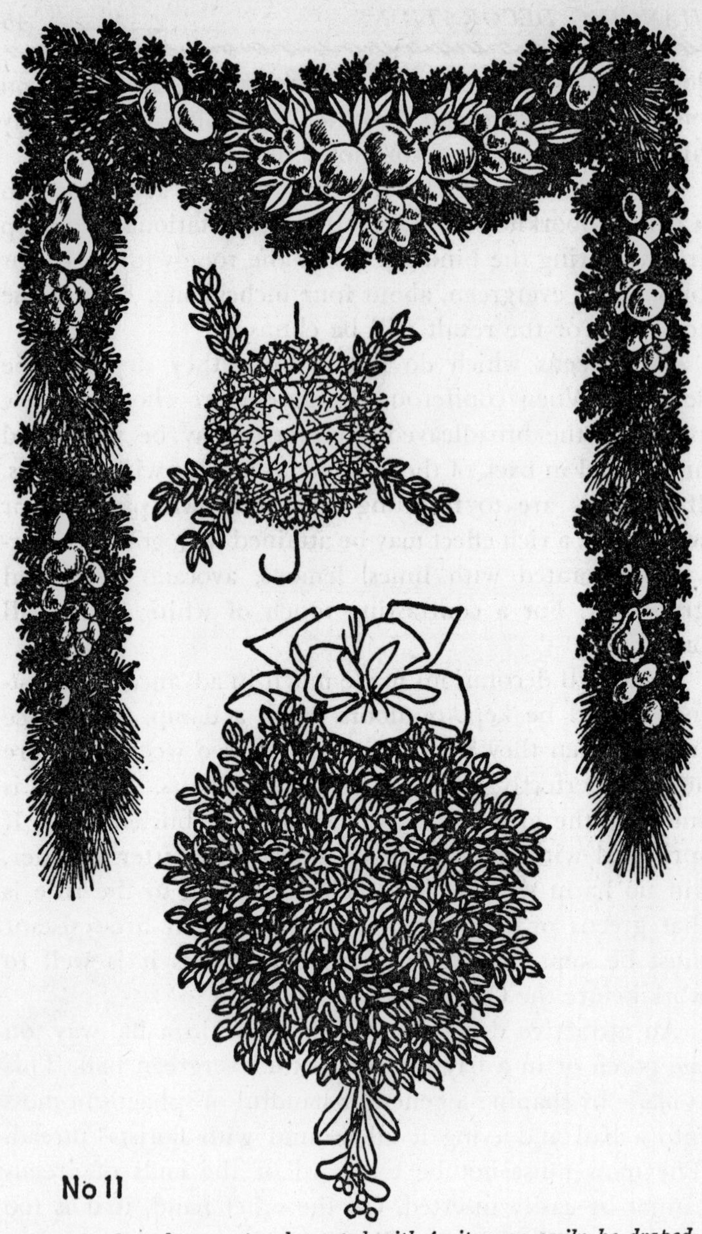

A garland made on rope, decorated with fruits may easily be draped. Sphagnum moss tied into a ball shape is filled with small pieces of boxwood. Mistletoe and a bow complete it for hanging.

Embroidery hoops and mistletoe are light to hang. Star ornaments hung from blue paper in deep doorways, or stars made from toothpicks inserted in corks and covered with glitter add sparkle to the room.

of needles and branches. If oblique cuts are made with shears, the ends are easy to poke in. Boxwood, yew, fir or spruce and some of the pines are all good for the ball because their wood is rigid and goes in easily. Hemlock and arborvitae may be more difficult to handle, depending on the size of the pieces. It is easier to make the ball if it is suspended on a wire. A 12-inch length can be inserted through the ball and hooked at the end to hold it. The top end can also be hooked and a ribbon may be fastened to this to suspend it. (Drawing 11) The ball may be decorated with berries, a red bow, bells or mistletoe. If mistletoe is used, it is called a kissing ball.

This type of decoration may be contrived with a pair of embroidery hoops fastened one within the other, at right angles, so that there are four equal sections. (Drawing 12) The hoops may be painted or wrapped with green ribbon or may be covered with small pieces of evergreens. Inside the ball a piece of mistletoe is suspended. This, too, is a kissing ball. It weighs so little it may be hung from lighting fixtures.

8 . . . Unique Designs for Artificial Trees

ARTIFICIAL TREES cannot compare with real Christmas trees in dignity or significance. They should be regarded as interesting fancies, or as decorative details in a complete Christmas picture. They may be created and used for special occasions, as for a children's party or a holiday dinner. In small homes or city apartments, where a real tree would be impractical, an artificial tree may serve as a symbol. It is better to have a tin tree, a wooden tree, a gumdrop or lollipop tree than no tree at all.

A simple artificial tree for flat surfaces was described in the preceding chapter. The trees we now consider stand alone, on tables or mantles or wide window sills. It would be difficult to supply clear instructions for making them without the help of pictures, so it is suggested that the reader glance first at Drawings 13, 14, 15, 16 and 21. Reference will be made below to individual drawings as each tree is discussed.

One of my favorites is the tin tree (Drawing 13). It is built on a wooden base about 8½ inches in diameter. A dowel stick or slender wooden rod, 18 inches high, is used for the trunk of the tree. This trunk is held in position by driving a nail through the bottom of the base board into the dowel stick, a job best done in a bench vise, or by a handy man. The spiral (Drawing 13) consists of an inch-wide strip of tin, 56 inches long. A substitute for tin is the metal binding which is sold by the yard for fastening carpets or linoleum to the floor.

An 18 inch dowel fastened to wooden base, 56 inches of inch wide tin, and star form the frame for the tin tree. Stubby pieces of evergreen hold fresh fruits in place.

It has neither the strength nor sparkle of tin but will serve the purpose. Force a hole through the end of the tin strip with a nail; then drive an ordinary tack through the hole to fasten it to the board, setting the strip at an angle. Coil this three times around the trunk and tack it to the top end. A 4½-inch tin star may then be tacked on the top of the tree.

This is the foundation of the tin tree. Now comes an opportunity to use the stubby, coarse pieces of evergreen usually discarded by the decorator. These are poked into the tin spiral. Fresh fruit, supported by the stiff stems, is mounded in among them. An apple may be used on one side, balanced by an orange on the other. Plums, lemons and grapes are suitable, and white onions tucked in, here and there, add brightness.

After the fruits are in place, or during their placing, evergreen ends are worked in so that they extend beyond the tin spiral. (Drawing 13) This tree will last well for a week or more, depending on the soundness of the fruit and the room temperature. The tree should stand where it need not be moved, as the fruit is likely to slip if disturbed.

Children prefer the lollipop tree. (Drawing 14) This begins with a conical frame made of half-inch mesh wire. For an 18-inch tree a frame 12 inches high and 6 inches wide will be needed. After the frame has been carefully shaped, it can be tied together with small pieces of wire. For cutting the mesh wire, tin shears are best but an old pair of heavy scissors will do.

The frame is filled with wet sphagnum moss, well packed into the point. If the tree is to stand on a tray or plate, it will not be necessary to tie the moss at the bottom. A round red tray, extending well beyond the greens, makes an attractive colorful base.

Small pieces of mixed greens are inserted through the

Half inch mesh galvanized wire forms the cone shaped frame filled with wet sphagnum moss. Evergreens, cellophane wrapped lollipops and wired holly berries inserted in the moss decorate the tree. Effective on red tray.

wire and into the moss. They should be fairly uniform in length in order to give the finished tree a good shape. Boxwood, yew and the blue-green retinospora (Chamaecyparis pisifera squarrosa) offer pleasing variety. The blue-green lightens the darker foliage and adds much to the beauty of the tree.

Insert small round lollipops, clear-colored and wrapped in cellophane, into the tree. This can be done easily if 6-inch lengths of No. 18 wire are twisted to the ends of the lollipop sticks. Because the lollipops will be eaten something more must be added, perhaps small bunches of artificial holly berries. The top decoration may be berries, a lollipop, or both.

This solid decoration can be easily moved around on its tray. If you place it on the table as a centerpiece, balance it with large red candles, an inch and a half in diameter. These can be fastened to star-shaped glass holders by melting stubs of old candles in a can and pouring enough wax into the holders to give a firm red base.

The tree described looks well on a table set for ten or more. Smaller or larger trees, for other purposes, can be made in the same way with cones of different dimensions. Basic materials of the lollipop tree and of some others mentioned can be kept from year to year. Store away both cones and moss.

It is interesting to devise variations on the basic idea with small pine and spruce cones, or cones in graduated sizes from large ones at the bottom to tiny fir and hemlock cones at the top. These are wired, as described before, and the wires thrust through the mesh into the moss. Cone trees are more formal than lollipop trees. A circle of red Christmas balls around the bottom adds elegance. Small clusters of berries, such as firethorn (Pyracantha) may cover the tree completely, or other fruits may be wired

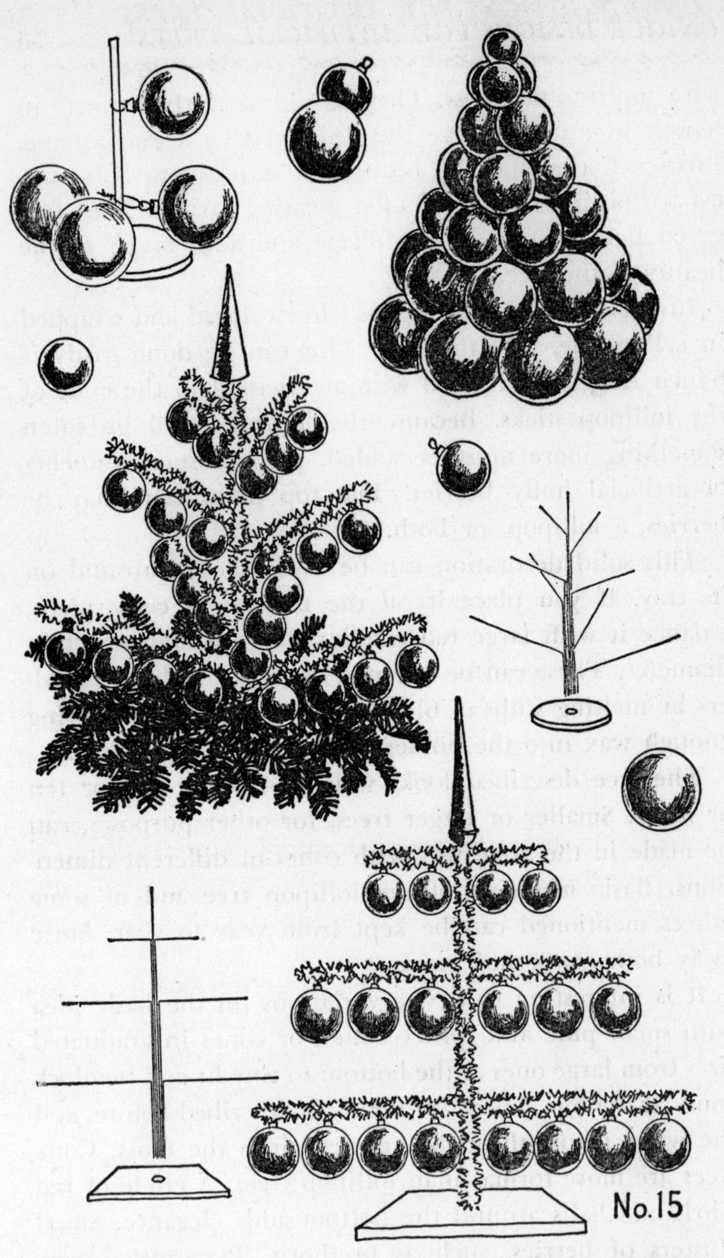

Christmas balls on a wire stem form a pyramid. Heavy wires are stapled to wooden base; arms and scotch tape hold balls in position; tinsel adds sparkle and conceals tape; greens decorate the base.

and inserted among greens. The foundation of the tree is still wire mesh, but decorations vary.

The wooden tree takes more time but is well within the ability of an amateur carpenter. Finished, it stands 18 inches high, plus 4½ inches for the star. Side pieces of the triangle (as shown in Drawing 16, middle), are 1¾ inches wide, ¾ of an inch thick and 16 inches long. The bottom of the triangle is 2 inches wide, ¾ of an inch thick and 15 inches long. Corners are neatly mitred. The base of the tree is cut from a block of wood 3 inches thick, 3 inches high and 6 inches long. The triangular frame sits in this curved base, which adds grace to the tree. A simpler platform may be made by fastening a block to each side of the triangle, with another piece nailed on the bottom for the stand.

Thickness through the base allows space for a shallow container to hold water for the greens. A sardine can will do. A flower holder hidden by the can holds greens or decorations firmly in place. The entire tree should be given two coats of aluminum paint. Then it is decorated with greens, tiny red balls, red berries and bayberry. Red candles are fastened to the sides on pieces of tin tacked to the frame. As explained above, holes are made in the tin with a nail before tacking, since a tack is not strong enough to pierce tin. A little adhesive tape is wrapped around the tin candle holders and the candles are fastened on with drops of melted wax. Greens must be kept within the frame at a safe distance from the candle flames. This tree makes a handsome centerpiece if decorated similarly on both sides. If only one side is covered, it must be placed against a suitable background.

As a variation, the wooden tree may be dressed with white berries, silver balls and white candles or a blue and silver scheme devised with artificial materials. Sprays of marble-size Christmas balls in groups or used singly are

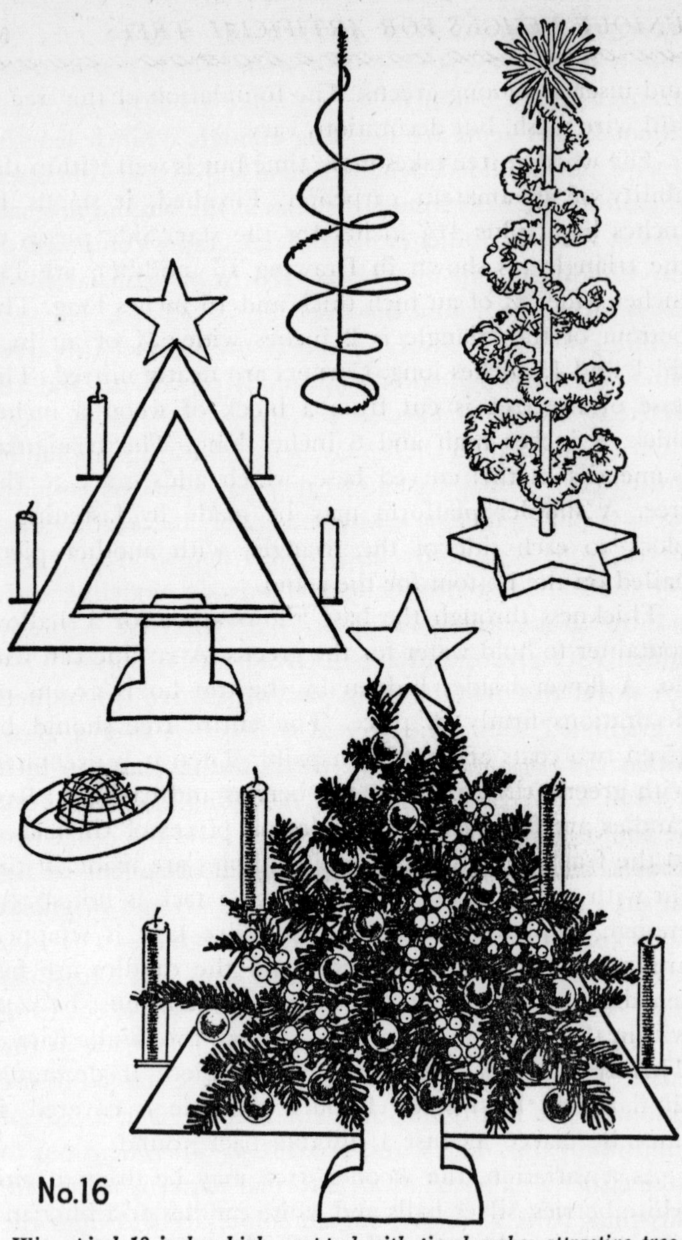

Wire spiral 18 inches high wrapped with tinsel makes attractive tree. Wooden frame with candles may be decorated with greens, berries and balls arranged in holder with water, or artificial materials may be used.

arranged in the flower holder to make an attractive decoration. If the stems are not long enough, 12-inch lengths of wire may be added. Symmetry and stability are obtained by grading the balls from large ones at the bottom to small ones at the top. Bunches of artificial grapes composed of tiny Christmas balls may be worked in or artificial silver leaves tucked in around the base.

Blue candles are lovely placed at the sides of this tree. When they are lighted, the gleam is picked up and reflected by the ornaments on the tree.

On a wide mantel there may be space for other candles at each end. A striking effect can be attained by employing as a candle holder, a kitchen grater, the kind with a curved front of uniform holes and a flat, solid tin back. The candle is fastened in melted wax or modeling clay, and the grater placed over it. Bases may be partially hidden with greens and cones. (Drawing 17, bottom)

A novel tree may be contrived with three tin funnels of graduated sizes. The largest is inverted over a glass, so that the rim of the funnel clears the table by an inch or two. A little Scotch tape or modeling clay will keep the funnel from slipping on the glass. Add the other two funnels, and then a Christmas tree-top ornament or tin star on a stick. Surround the tree with silvered magnolia leaves for an attractive modernistic design.

Other trees can be made of wire arms and Christmas balls. (Drawing 15) A base of convenient size is cut from the side of an orange crate and an inch hole made in the center. Two-foot lengths of No. 10 wire are stapled to the bottom of the board and then the base is given a coat of aluminum paint. The wires, or arms, are then bent out to make either a balanced or an informal pattern, as desired. Christmas balls in one or mixed colors are slid onto the wire arms and firmed with strips of Scotch tape. Tinsel may be coiled around the arms or bits of evergreens attached by wires. A star or pointed tree ornament finishes the top. These decorations are brilliant in large hallways or dark corners of the house. They are not difficult to store, since the balls may be removed from their hooks and returned to boxes.

Another type of ball tree may be quickly assembled on an upright piece of heavy wire inserted through the center of a suitable wooden base and firmly stapled. Then balls of graduated sizes and mixed colors are threaded on the heavy wire. (Drawing 15, top) The base may be concealed by silvered magnolia leaves or pieces of white pine brushed with silver paint.

Silver or gold dust, purchased at art stores, is a substitute for paint. The dust flakes off, as paint does not, but some decorators prefer the subtler effect. To coat leaves or cones, paint them with thin glue. Then drop them into a paper bag of gold or silver dust. Close tightly and shake thoroughly. Allow the dust to settle for a few minutes before removing leaves and cones now ready for use. So treated they may adorn wreaths, sprays or garlands.

Half the end of an orange crate makes a good base for another artificial tree. No holes need be drilled for this one. A piece of wood 1 inch thick and 2 inches wide, of any desired height, is nailed perpendicularly to the broad side of the crate section, or to any other suitable piece of wood. The perpendicular piece serves as the trunk of the tree. To this graduated branches are stapled, first on one side, then on the other. The base board prevents the tree from pitching forward; it can be painted, or concealed by a covering of greens and a mound of Christmas balls. This type of tree can be easily and inexpensively made for mantels and tables, or for the decoration of halls and churches.

Another novelty is the wire spiral tree. This is made by twisting four 18-inch lengths of No. 18 wire together to make a continuous piece. A small coil is formed at the base and 2 inches of straight wire left above the coil to serve as the tree's trunk. Then the spiral begins. Another 18-inch wire is fastened to the trunk and the spiral attached to its top. (Drawing 16, top)

Set the wire coil at the bottom of the tree into plaster of Paris, the base of most artificial trees, since it is cheap, easy to mix and adaptable. In a few minutes the plaster sets and becomes firm. To facilitate thorough drying, place it on something like a needle-point holder which will permit air to reach the bottom. After standing overnight the base is dry enough to place on fine furniture without danger of moisture affecting the wood.

The spiral tree that has its base, stands alone and is easy to decorate. There are many kinds of rope tinsel. Some are metallic, some made of tinfoil, some of cellophane. The spiral is wrapped with one of these and a star placed at the top.

Lightweight trees such as these are charming on mantels, in hallways and at the ends of long dinner tables with a heavier low decoration for centerpiece. The frame can be kept from year to year and given fresh adornment. It is amazing how different tinsels change the appearance of the tree. For variety, hang tiny balls from the spiral. The tinsel will keep them from slipping.

The base for an 18-inch tree requires several tablespoonfuls of plaster of Paris. Mix this with warm water in a tin can. Stir constantly to prevent quick hardening. The amount of water needed varies with the quality and brand of the plaster; some kinds take longer to harden than others. A little vinegar may be added to retard the setting of the plaster but warm water serves almost as well. Some experimenting should be done to determine right proportions.

Do not put the plaster into the water or it may crumble

after it has set. When the right mixture is ready, pour it on brown paper, as if making hot cakes. Insert the wire of the tree at once and hold it for a few minutes until the plaster becomes firm. If the mixture is soft and runs away from the center, poke it back with a spoon so that the base is no more than 5 inches in diameter. It may be sprinkled with artificial snow while it is still wet, or painted with silver after it dries. The plaster of Paris base will be found useful for other decorations, not only for Christmas, but for anniversaries and festivities throughout the year.

Branches of huckleberry or the twiggy growth of the pepperidge tree (Nyssa sylvatica) can be arranged effectively in plaster. Tie the branches at the bottom with white string; colored string is likely to run in the plaster. Insert the branches and hold in place until the plaster sets. The branches may be whitened with a casein paint or with home-made snow (Chapter 5). This decoration looks well against a tilt-top table or other dark background.

The gumdrop tree is always popular, particularly with children, though I have never demonstrated it to adults who did not find it enchanting. This tree requires the branches of some thorny wood, such as hawthorn. Small gumdrops, more or less round, and slender spice drops are impaled on the thorns. As with huckleberry or pepperidge branches, the twigs are set in a plaster base and painted white with casein or quick-drying enamel. A glitter of snow on the wet paint adds a delicate sparkle. Candies are added when the paint is dry. Care should be taken in grouping the twigs to insure even distribution of thorns. On these depends the spacing of the candies. (Drawing 24)

A variation is the tree decorated with cranberries. These are effective on whitened branches with a few twigs of yew among them. First-size, quality berries should be selected. A coat of shellac will increase their luster and help preserve and hold them. (Drawing 21)

The confetti tree can be built of any branches, set in plaster and covered with white paint, glue or shellac. Confetti is then poured on. If it sticks unevenly, bad spots can be touched up. Miniatures of this tree are suitable for favors which children enjoy making.

Painted branches can be used in many ways. Tiny balls, bells, gummed paper stars and small bunches of cellophane straws can be fastened to them. The straws are most effective if their ends are cut on a slant to taper them. The ends may be dabbed with white paint and sprinkled with silver glitter, or wired artificial holly berries may be inserted in the end of each straw. A bend in the wire holds them in place.

Any thick branches of trees or shrubs can be made decorative by these methods. Good effects are possible with sumac (Rhus), the corky twigs of euonymus (Euonymus alatus) or sweet gum (Liquidambar styraciflua). Fasten them in a base, then swish them around in a thick mixture of clothes starch, sprinkle with artificial snow and allow to dry. A needle-point holder will serve as base. Artificial leaves or flowers can be added.

There are endless possibilities in this field of decoration. Artificial trees can be made for any color scheme or space. They are fascinating to contrive when the simple tricks of the trade are mastered.

9 . . . Decorating with Candles

CANDLES ARE popular throughout the year, but at no other season do we find such varied sizes and shapes as at Christmas. Decorative in themselves, they sometime present problems as to holders. For very large ones, angel candles or other irregular forms, mirrors, red glass plates or old china plates, painted red, make pleasing bases. Small pieces of evergreens may be clustered around them or whitened twigs and berries tied to them with a bow kept at safe distance from the flame. (Drawing 17) A wooden base, of the flower-arrangement type, makes an excellent stand. Melted wax or modeling clay will hold the candle in place or a nail may even be driven through the bottom to serve as a spike on which to impale the candle.

The candle bowl is easy to arrange and a safe way to burn a candle. (Drawing 17, top) Any clear glass bowl, fish aquarium or battery jar, will serve as container. Fasten the candle, which should not extend beyond the top of the bowl, in the center of the bottom with melted wax or modeling clay. Then drop around the candle, in the bowl, small pieces of greens and for brightness a few red and silver balls. The effect is surprising and the heat of the candle will not crack the bowl. This is a safe way to burn candles in the window, on the hall table where there is apt to be a draft, or on the center of the dining table.

This same idea may be carried out in miniature for individual favors by using baby food jars and large-size birthday-cake candles. To make a steady base for these,

No. 17

Fish aquarium or berry bowl makes safe enclosure for candle. Greens and balls add color and sparkle. Large candles are effective on stands, mirrors and behind tin kitchen graters. Greens ornament base.

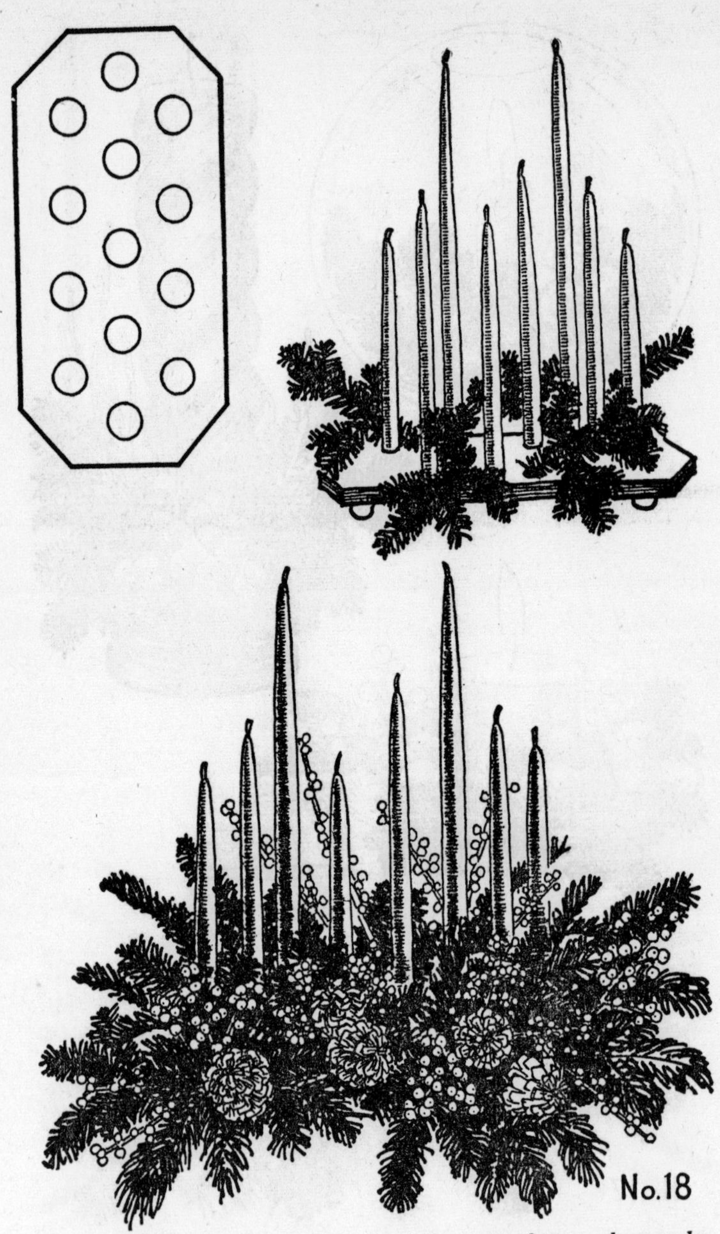

Board of desired length, candle size holes properly spaced, may be decorated in many ways with candles, greens, cones, berries, fruits or Christmas balls.

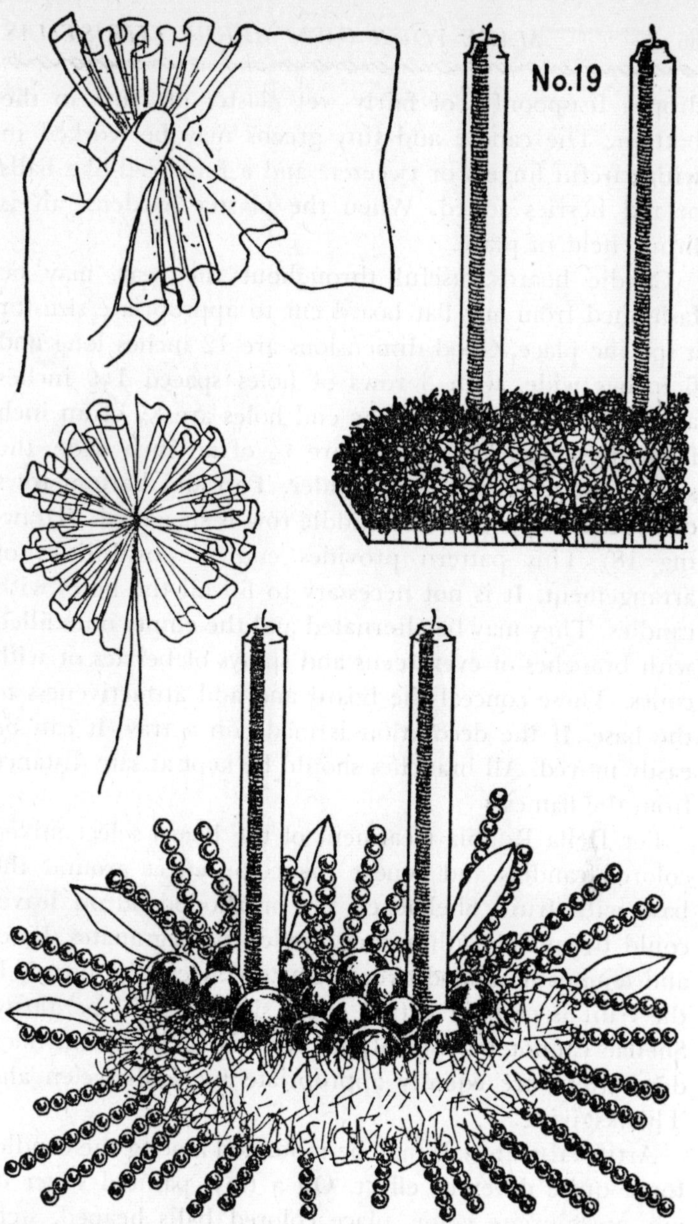

Large candles fastened in dry sphagnum moss-packed board, covered with white crêpe paper, forms base for wired cellophane pompons and Christmas balls.

drop a teaspoonful of fairly wet plaster of Paris in the bottom. The candle and tiny greens may be worked in with careful fingers or tweezers and a few bead-like balls or red berries added. When the plaster hardens, all is firmly held in place.

Candle boards, useful throughout the year, may be fashioned from any flat board cut to appropriate size for a specific place. Good dimensions are 12 inches long and 6 inches wide, with 3 rows of holes spaced 1½ inches apart. In the center row the end holes are ¾ of an inch from the edge. These holes are ⅞ of an inch wide, the size of the average candle holder. Top and bottom rows of holes are opposite; the middle row is staggered. (Drawing 18) This pattern provides endless possibilities of arrangement. It is not necessary to fill all the holes with candles. They may be alternated and the empty ones filled with branches of evergreens and sprays of berries or with cones. These conceal the board and add attractiveness to the base. If the decoration is made on a tray, it can be easily moved. All branches should be kept at safe distance from the flames.

For Della Robbia treatment of the board select mixed colored candles and repeat the color effect around the base with fruit. Shellacked ivy or rhododendron leaves could be spread with grapes, apples, pomegranates, limes and lemons mounded over them to conceal the board. If the fruit is painted with a sugar sirup, it will be glossy. Shellac cannot be used if the fruit is to be eaten. Such decorations are equally appropriate for Hallowe'en and Thanksgiving.

Artificial materials may be mounded among the candles for a quite different effect. On a tray, painted silver or any appropriate color, place colored balls heaped, stem side down, around white candles. Crumpled silver paper beneath the balls will keep them from rolling and, if necessary, add height. The ends of the tray may be finished with silver bells or small artificial silver trees, all available at the holiday season. This makes an attractive centerpiece or mantel decoration.

The decoration of candle boards may be considerably varied. Large candles, one and a half inches in diameter, need special boards, or they may be worked into moss bases. If boards are made, holes should be fewer and farther apart. The heat from the candles will cause them to melt if they are too close to one another. Different effects may be achieved by gilding or silvering leaves, cones and greens and by rubbing candles with a piece of absorbent cotton dipped in gilt, silver or bronze dust.

One or two wires or pieces of dark green string, tied around the board, will hold greens in place. The ends of some of the pieces may be kept in position by slipping them under the wire. As soon as a few are firmed others may easily be put on.

Sphagnum moss is indispensable for bases into which wires or stems have to be inserted. Here a soft medium is needed and the moss is ideal. Bread pans may be filled with wet sphagnum moss, securely tied over the top and around the pan. Evergreen stems are cut obliquely and inserted into the moss with sprays of berries for decoration. The greens and berries can be arranged to hang over the side or extend along the edge to conceal the pan. This may be set on an inconspicuous tray or piece of waxed paper to prevent the soiling of a tablecloth. A candle may be placed as a center feature at the time the moss is being packed and before it is tied in position. The moss-filled pan makes a steady holder.

Candles may also become the feature of the cellophane decoration shown in Drawing 19. For this, dry sphagnum moss is mounded on a piece of cardboard cut to desired size and shape, usually an oblong about the size of the candle board. First the candles are held in the desired position. Very often I pack the moss around them. Then I remove them while I tie on the moss and reset them later. They can always be firmed in place with a little more moss. After this is tied, it is covered with white crepe paper rather than with tissue which tears easily. The crepe paper is fastened together on the bottom with Scotch tape. Candles are then set in place, and wired cellophane pompons and artificial balls inserted in the moss. Pompons are made by gathering, through the center, cellophane pieces of the desired size as shown in Drawing 19. The 12-inch length of No. 18 or No. 20 wire is twisted so that two hairpin-like pieces extend out the back. These are thrust through the paper into the moss to hold the pompons in place. This decoration, icy in appearance, is effective where heavy greens and dark colors are not.

In Drawing 21 another decoration is shown. This was made with crepe paper, moss base, a white brush tree at one side, cellophane pompons around the edge and white reindeer across the top. Before the reindeer were placed, the crepe paper on the top was covered with absorbent cotton or glass wool to simulate snow. Whitened twigs behind the trees add beauty and height. It may be necessary to fasten a small wire around one leg of each reindeer to hold it in place.

10 . . . *All Through the House*

FLOWER BOXES at the window or on the porch are charming decorated for the holidays. They may be filled with sprays of evergreens and berries. If suet is added, birds will be attracted to the boxes and be a delight to watch from inside the house.

In the hallway, an old lantern of considerable size might occupy a table. If this is lighted by electricity, berries and greens can be placed inside the lantern as well as around the outside. (Drawing 20) If a candle has to be used, then the decorations should only be placed outside on the table. Very thick candles which will burn for hours are available.

From the tops of deep doorways or windows, stars may be hung from a sky of blue paper. Or this idea may be carried out in an entrance hall, under a small roof over the front door or in the ceiling of a bay window. The paper is fastened with Scotch tape and the star-like ornaments secured to the paper with tree hooks. These stars twinkle and sparkle when the air moves and people circulate through the rooms. Other gummed stars may be pasted flat on the surface to increase the effect. (Drawing 12, top)

Stars of all kinds are appropriate to Christmas. Homemade ones may be suspended in the hallway or from the moulding over the doorway. (Drawing 12) They may also be used to decorate a mantel and carry the star effect through an entire room. The stars in Drawing 12 were made by inserting cocktail toothpicks into corks. These toothpicks come in many colors. They are stronger than ordinary ones and have two pointed ends which make them easy to insert. A cork about three quarters of an

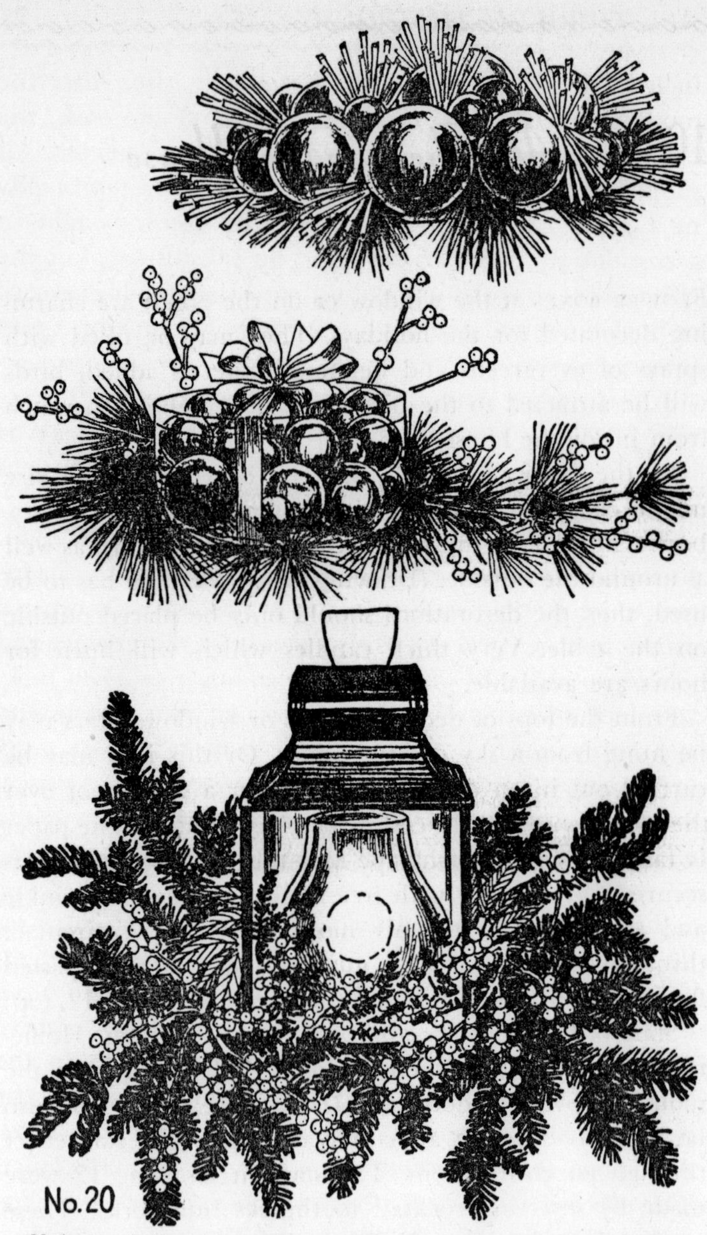

Christmas balls, evergreens and cellophane straws arranged on tray or balls in cellophane box make gay centerpieces. Old carriage house lantern, wired for safety, is attractive in hallway with greens and berries.

inch thick and an inch wide is the right size. After the toothpicks have been inserted all around the cork, the finished star will be about 4½ inches in diameter. All should be brushed with glue and then shaken thoroughly in a paper bag of silver decorettes or glitter bought in a costume store. Silver dust may be substituted, but the effect is not so sparkling. A thin wire fastened in the cork or hooked around one toothpick makes the ornament easy to suspend.

A few similar stars placed among evergreens will decorate a mantel. Wooden or glass star-like holders may be used for the greens with modeling clay to hold the stems in place. (Drawing 12)

The fireplace offers great possibilities for decoration. In itself it is always a feature of the room and at Christmas more so than ever. For the mantel two tin cans of proper size are selected. Given a coat of red enamel and placed on a pair of black bases, they are filled with pine, yew, leucothoe, laurel and some red berries to add beauty and distinction to the mantel. The same principles apply to Christmas decorations, of course, as to flower arrangements. We must consider balance, proportion, harmony and other elements if we wish to be successful. (Drawing 22, center)

The yule log theme of the fireplace can be repeated on the mantel by the use of cork bark. It is light in weight, clean, and does not fall apart. Often a small curved piece is obtainable and can be used as a container for a simple and effective decoration. Wedge a white potato in the bark or a whole or a part of a loaf of bread. Then insert the stems of a few pieces of fir, pine, chamaecyparis and laurel. Add sprays of red berries to one side and white to the other. The effect of this yule log container is appropriate for the season. (Drawing 22, bottom)

If the log does not have a natural curve, it may be soaked in water, curved when soft, tied into the desired

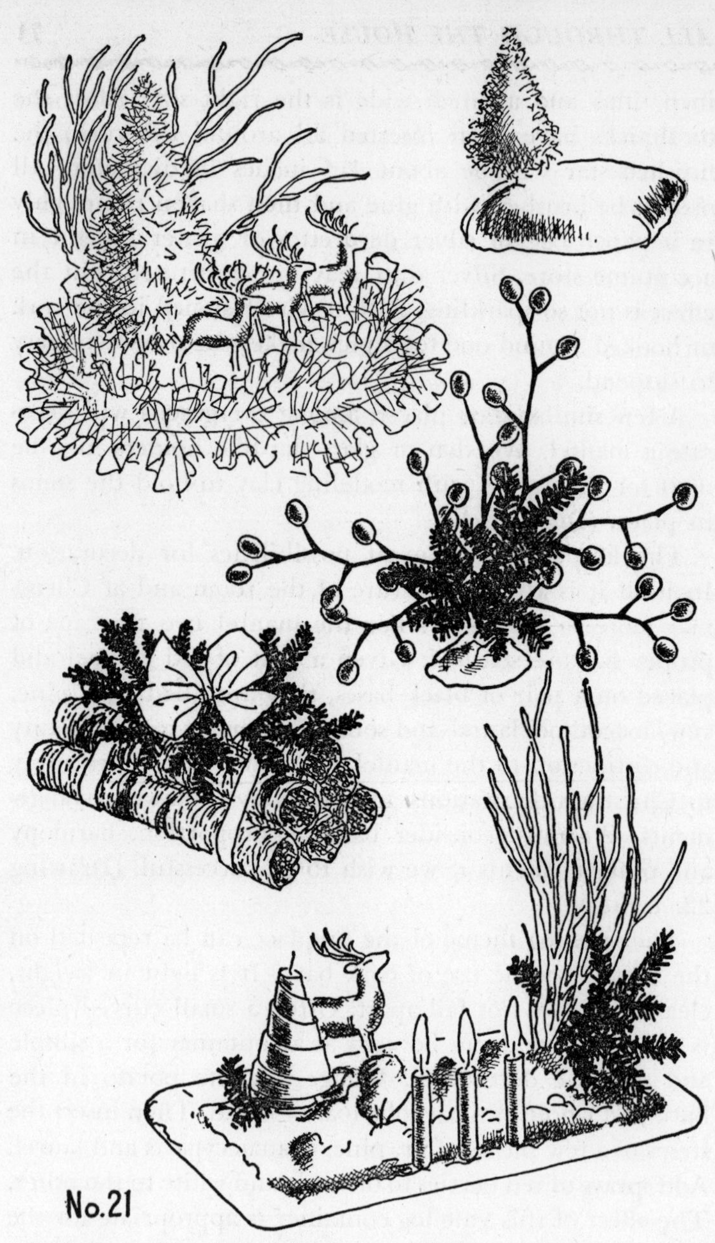

Decoration with reindeer, brush tree, cellophane pompons, is made on base similar to plate 19. Yarn and greens brighten fagots. Cranberries impaled on hawthorne twigs, and arrangement on tray are held in position in plaster of Paris.

shape and left until thoroughly dry. It will then hold its shape permanently. If any weight is needed to keep the bark from rolling, a needle-point flower holder or piece of lead may be placed inside. The log can always be held in position with a piece of Scotch tape which will not mar the mantel or furniture.

Bark will keep indefinitely and should be stored for future use. Each year its decoration may be varied. A few greens and cones placed alone in a bark container are beautiful or artificial snowballs may be wired among them.

Angels are beautiful symbols of the season. They come in many colors and are made of wax, pottery, wood, china and glass. They may be used singly or grouped on a mantel, window sill or table center with greens, or placed on a side table around a small tree.

Cones, driftwood and fagots may be prepared for the fireplace with little effort after materials are assembled. Different treatments produce colored flames. A solution of chemicals can be used but dipping requires a wooden container and more time and space than sprinkling with chemicals. A large salt or flour shaker is convenient to scatter these over a surface which has been brushed with shellac or glue in order to make the chemicals adhere. Colored flames are produced as follows

Yellow .... Sodium chloride (salt) and Potassium nitrate
Red .... Lithium chloride and Strontium nitrate
Green .... Copper nitrate
Blue .... Copper sulphate
Orange .... Calcium chloride
Violet .... Potassium chloride

Prepared driftwood crystals may also be bought for this purpose.

Many trees such as the plane and some of the birches in the East and eucalyptus in the West shed their bark. If curved pieces can be found, they make nice coverings

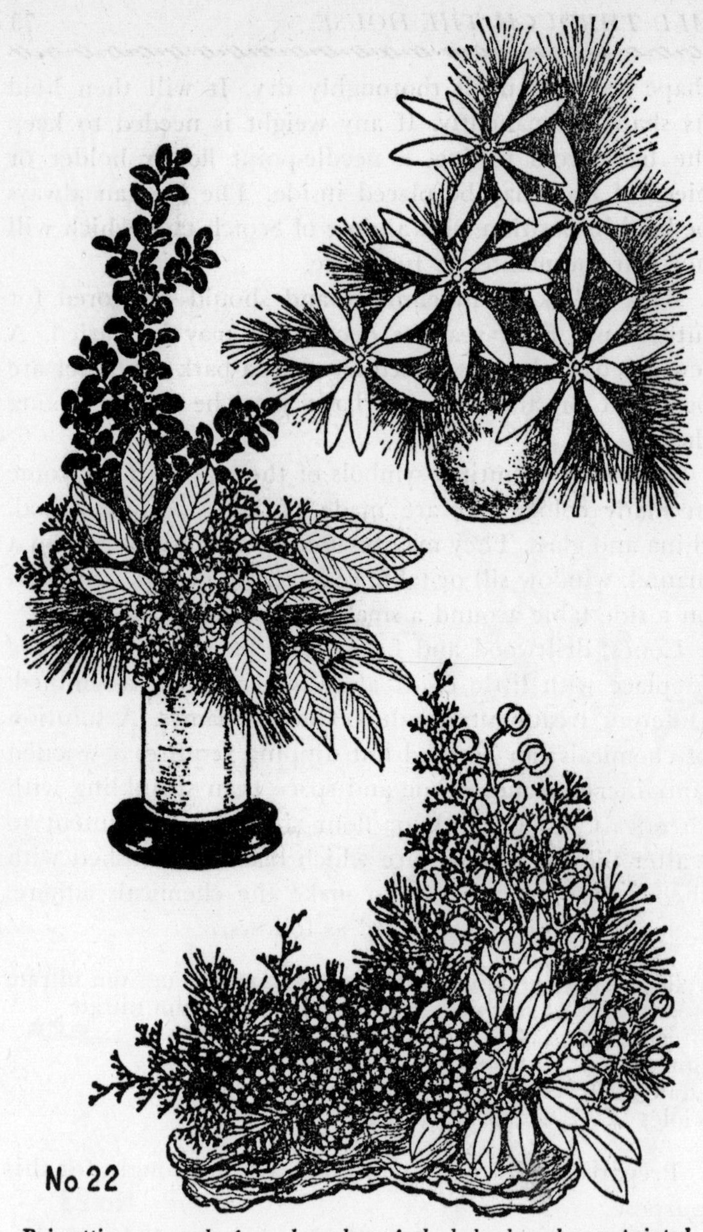

Poinsettias are made from branches of rhododendron leaves painted red. Painted tin can on base serves as container for greens and berries. Cork bark is light weight and effective as yule log container.

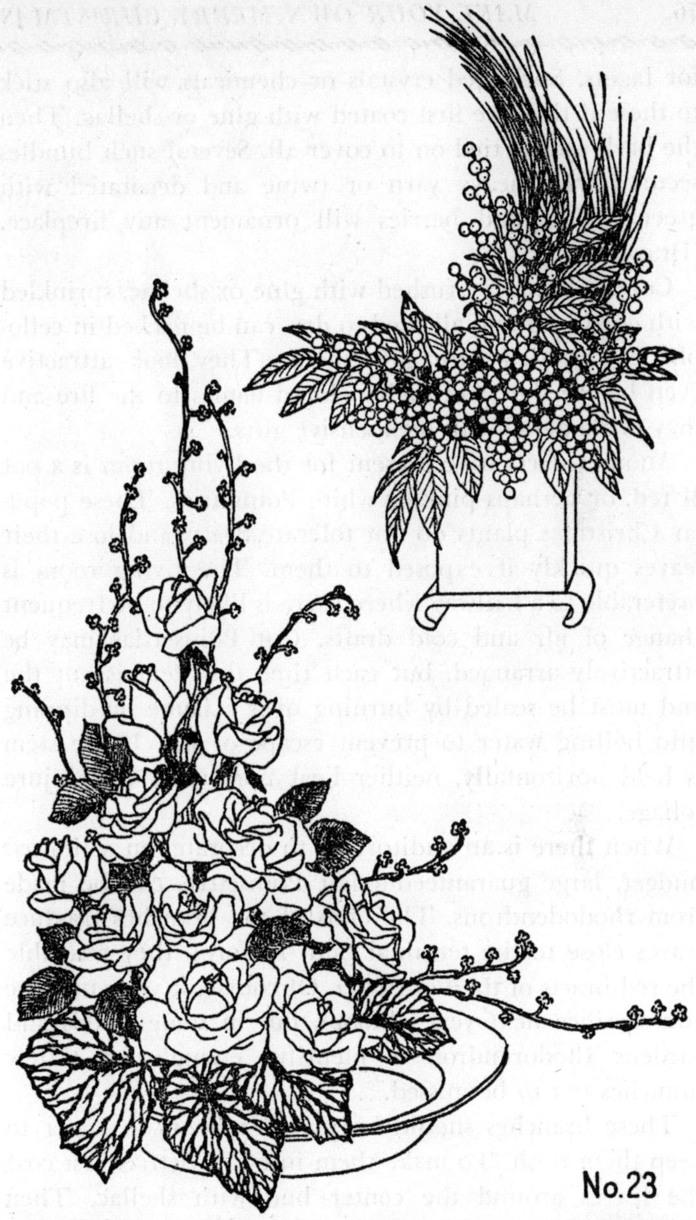

Scotch broom, berries, leucothoe or other evergreens are attractive in Chinese pewter container. Red roses, twigs and begonia leaves make interesting arrangement for buffet party or any occasion.

for fagots. Sprinkled crystals or chemicals will also stick to these if they are first coated with glue or shellac. Then the bark can be tied on to cover all. Several such bundles secured with heavy yarn or twine and decorated with greens, cones and berries will ornament any fireplace. (Drawing 21)

Cones, similarly brushed with glue or shellac, sprinkled with chemicals and allowed to dry, can be packed in cellophane bags tied with gay ribbon. They look attractive even before they add their colored flames to the fire and they make delightful, inexpensive gifts.

Another decorative present for the living room is a pot of red, or perhaps pink or white Poinsettias. These popular Christmas plants do not tolerate drafts and lose their leaves quickly if exposed to them. The living room is preferable to a hallway where there is likely to be frequent change of air and cold drafts. Cut Poinsettias may be attractively arranged, but each time the stem is cut the end must be sealed by burning over a flame or dipping into boiling water to prevent escape of sap. If the stem is held horizontally, neither heat nor steam will injure foliage.

When there is an auditorium to decorate, on a limited budget, large guaranteed-to-last Poinsettias can be made from rhododendrons. The ends of the branches produce leaves close to the terminal bud. In form, they resemble the red bracts of the Poinsettia. Of course, if you cut these you sacrifice next year's bloom, but in some woods and gardens rhodorendron is plentiful enough for a few branches not to be missed.

These branches should be placed indoors in water to keep them fresh. To make them into Poinsettias first coat the leaves around the center bud with shellac. Then paint with flat show-card red. If enamel is used, shellac is not necessary. Enamel lasts well and will not flake off, but it does not look so genuine as flat red. To make a realistic flower center, cut the pointed rhododendron bud in half and paint with show-card or yellow enamel. The flowers in Drawing 22 were made this way.

In the library, or for the table at the top of the steps, there are many interesting possibilities. Attractive Christmas balls with broken hook ends need not be discarded. They may be inverted on hyacinth stakes or twigs and arranged in a flower holder. Evergreens tucked among them will create a pleasing effect.

An old tray or an inexpensive new one may support the plaster of Paris base of another amusing arrangement. (Drawing 21, bottom) To create a rough base surface, cinders or crumpled wet newspapers may be used. Either will reduce the amount of plaster needed. Whitened twigs may be set in the background, a reindeer or two placed in it and one or more candles inserted in the front at safe distance from the twigs. A thin mixture of plaster of Paris is poured over the cinder base to hold everything in place. While it is wet, it may be sprinkled with artificial snow. This makes an attractive hall decoration or centerpiece.

Small trays or red plates may be made up in the same way. Fasten a red glass in the center or at the side, fill it with water to keep the nicely arranged greens fresh, and then place small birds, ducks, reindeer or any other small animals. Santa Claus candles can also be inserted in the plaster of Paris. A steady decoration made this way can easily be transported to a neighbor or sick friend. With a long board as base a complete snow or skating scene may be set up depending on the figures available. Bits of evergreens make fine trees. Mirrors look like ponds. Rock candy resembles chunks of ice. Such decorations may occupy a whole window sill, the top of an upright piano or a mantel with red candle trees at the ends.

For the dining room table many decorations have been suggested of real and artificial materials. Some take a lot of time, others very little. The busy housewife, or the one who does not like to fashion her own trees and wreaths, may take Christmas balls and arrange them on a silver tray for a truly effective centerpiece. To prevent the balls from rolling about, a few pieces of some such evergreen as cedar or arborvitae may be added as well as bunches of cellophane straws. The difference in form adds interest to the piece. (Drawing 20)

A cellophane box in which an orchid corsage was received may be filled with balls of various size, tied with a red satin bow and placed on a foundation of greens and berries. (Drawing 20) The effect is excellent for so little effort. Both of these decorations may be elaborated upon.

Fresh cut flowers are always a delight. Red roses, red carnations and many others may be attractively arranged with bronzy pieces of leucothoe, begonia foliage, galax or other leaves. A few deciduous branches may be included for form and height. (Drawing 23) In order to insure their lasting, the flowers should be set in a cool place at night. Certain materials sold to prolong the life of cut flowers do help, as will a pinch of complete fertilizer added to the water. Fresh cuts should be made on the ends of the stems each time they are rearranged, and warm water used in preference to cold. This will expel air from stems and allow more moisture to be absorbed.

For those who do not care to buy fresh foliage through the winter, and yet like to use it during the holidays, there is a way of preserving fall leaves, especially those of the beech. While sap is still flowing, but leaves are turning yellow and brown, branches may be cut and the stems placed in a mixture of one-third water and two-thirds glycerin. Water may be added if some evaporates. This solution will keep beech leaves indefinitely. With their beautiful rich sheen they make pleasing backgrounds for nut and fruit arrangements and are a charming contrast to greens.

11 . . . Christmas Tables and Favors

THE SNOW WHITE damask cloth, regarded by many as old-fashioned, is still my choice for the Christmas dinner table. It serves as a fine background to the well-browned turkey, the dark red cranberries, the burning plum pudding, and the mixed candies and nuts.

Gay colored cloths and table coverings can be made for Christmas Eve, Christmas breakfast or supper and the many holiday parties. For these occasions, innumerable ideas can be carried out with red sateen, ribbon, cellophane, brocade, metal-cloth and materials of different colors to blend with the color scheme of the room or china. The cloth may be weighted at the corners with bells and tiny ones fastened in one corner of each napkin to add to the gaiety of the table.

A distinctive effect for the mahogany table top between meals may be created by arranging broad bands of red or green satin ribbon as if tying a package. Where they cross there may be a large bow, an arrangement of greens or candles.

The main points to remember with tables are to keep the decorations in proportion to the size of the table and the room and to carry out a definite color scheme. Cluttered, poorly proportioned decorations without definite color schemes lack distinction.

Much of the food we serve on the table can be made more festive with little additional effort. The fruit cup, garnished with a red cherry, can be placed in grapefruit baskets made from the shell of half a grapegruit and tied with red ribbon. (Drawing 24) Salads and cookies may

Card board roll covered with Christmas paper, filled with wrapped hard candies, star shape candle, gum drop tree and Santa made from fruits and vegetables, are party favors. Grapefruit basket is used for fruit cup.

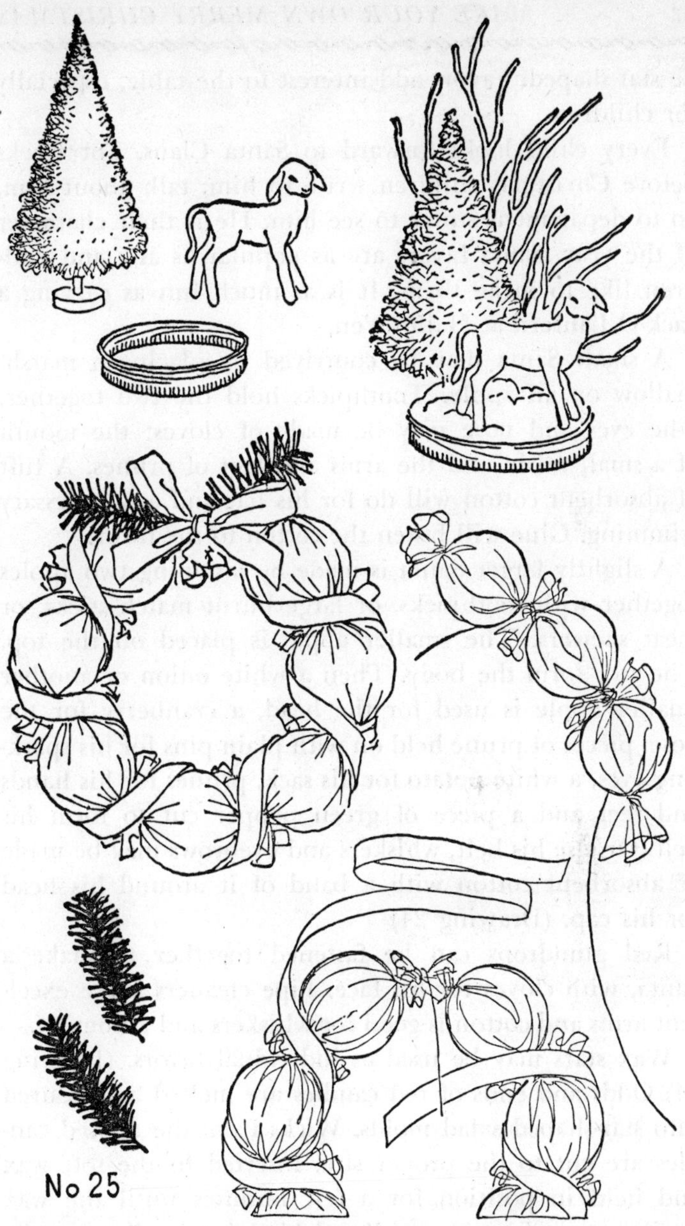

Tiny tree, greens, doe, berries, etc., are arranged in plaster of Paris in lid of peanut butter jar. Candy wreath is made by wiring seven uniform, wrapped hard candies together. Ribbon and greens add finish.

be star-shaped. Favors add interest to the table, especially for children.

Every child looks forward to Santa Claus. For weeks before Christmas children write to him, talk about him, go to department stores to see him. He is their character of the year. Santa favors are as popular as any and children like to make them. It is as much fun as carving a Jack-O-Lantern at Hallowe'en.

A small Santa may be contrived by placing a marshmallow on an apple. Toothpicks hold the two together. The eyes and nose may be made of cloves; the mouth of a small raisin and the arms and feet of prunes. A tuft of absorbent cotton will do for his hat and any necessary trimming. Glue will fasten the cotton to the favor.

A slightly larger Santa is made by fastening two apples together with toothpicks, or large burnt match sticks, or meat skewers. The smaller apple is placed on the top. The two form the body. Then a white onion or another smaller apple is used for the head, a cranberry for the nose, pieces of prune held on with plain pins for his sparkling eyes, a white potato for his sack, prunes for his hands and feet and a piece of green pepper cut to form his belt. Or else his belt, whiskers and eyebrows may be made of absorbent cotton with a band of it around his head for his cap. (Drawing 24)

Red gumdrops can be fastened together to make a Santa, with cloves for his face. Pipe cleaners make excellent arms and cotton is good for whiskers and trimming.

Wax stars may be used as individual favors. (Drawing 24) Odds and ends of red candles are melted and poured into star-shaped salad molds. Wicks from the melted candles are cut to the proper size, inserted in the soft wax and held in position for a few minutes until the wax begins to get firm, or small red birthday candles may be inserted for the wick. When firm, the wax forms drop from the mold. If there is difficulty in removing them, a warm cloth placed on the bottom will loosen them.

Favors may be made from the lids of peanut butter jars. In some cases these are already painted red, but if not they can be coated with red enamel. The favor is then made by filling the lid with a mixture of plaster of Paris, and quickly inserting a few sprigs of greens and berries with a small animal or Santa in the front. If kept in the cold, these will last for several weeks, so they can be made in advance. (Drawing 25)

Small candle bowls have been described previously in the chapter on candle decorations.

The candy wreath is a favorite. For this seven pieces of round, cellophane-wrapped hard candies are used. The twisted ends of the cellophane are overlapped and fastened together with No. 25 wire. The wire is carried around in one continuous piece. It will take more than one 12-inch length to fasten the seven candies together. Although not necessary, it does make a more attractive wreath if an 18- to 20-inch piece of narrow red ribbon is twisted around the wreath to cover the wire. This is tied at the top and a small piece of green fastened in the tie. (Drawing 25)

The hard candy roll delights children. It is made from an empty cardboard roll of paper towel or waxed paper, cut to size and covered with good pieces of discarded Christmas wrappings. These are fastened with Scotch tape or a Christmas seal. Enough paper is allowed for fraying the ends. This is usually done before fastening the paper on the roll. One end is tied with ribbon of appropriate color, the tube filled with wrapped hard candies, and the other end tied. These rolls, gay in appearance, are quickly made with materials otherwise worthless. (Drawing 24)

The Christmas corsage or nosegay is always popular. It should not be too large or it will look heavy. It may be fashioned with greens, berries, small bells or balls. Tip ends of andromeda (Pieris floribunda) resemble miniature balls and are decorative in form and color. The advantage of the corsage of greens is that it will last about a week, provided hemlock is not used. If flowers of the Christmas rose (Helleborus niger) can be obtained, they are certainly appropriate and I know of no flower that lasts longer or is more beautiful for wearing at this season. When the corsage is not in use, the stems should rest in water.

Place cards may be made in the form of small trees or wreaths. It may be possible to buy wreath stickers, or sketch a wreath around a picture of each person to be seated at the table. If old snapshots are used for this purpose, the place cards will be amusing conversation pieces and it is surprising how many will have difficulty in identifying themselves.

Plain white cards may be decorated at one end with greens and berries. A dab of plaster of Paris or Duco cement or glue may be used to fasten tiny ends of greens, hemlock cones and individual berries.

12 . . . *Favorite Recipes*

THE FOLLOWING carefully selected and tested recipes will add joy to holiday eating and drinking. In most cases they are suitable for any season of the year. All are old favorites of my family and friends.

CHRISTMAS PUNCH

2 cups strong tea
3/4 cup lemon juice
1 1/3 cups orange juice
2 tablespoons lime juice
1 cup sugar
Leaves from 12 sprigs of mint
8 slices of pineapple and juice from the can
4 pints ginger ale
4 pints plain soda
Crushed ice

Place tea in a large bowl, add and stir well the lemon, lime and orange juices and mint leaves. Place these ingredients on ice for two hours. Shortly before serving, strain the punch, add the pineapple slices and juice, ginger ale, soda and crushed ice. Serves eighteen.

DECORATED ICE CUBES FOR ICED DRINKS

Fill a refrigerator tray with water. Place in each section one of the following:

A maraschino cherry
A preserved strawberry
A piece of lemon or pineapple
A sprig of mint, if available

Freeze the water. Serve the cubes in punch, lemonade, tea or other cold drinks. The water may be colored and flavored.

FRUIT PUNCH

1 cup sugar
1 cup water
2 cups strong hot tea
3/4 cup crushed pineapple
5 lemons, juice only
5 oranges, juice only
2 cups strawberry, grape or other fruit juices
1 cup maraschino cherries
1 quart carbonated water

Boil the sugar and water together for ten minutes. Add the tea. Let this cool, then add the pineapple and fruit juices. Chill for about one hour, then add enough cold water to make four quarts in all. Just before serving add the carbonated water and cherries. Pour into tall glasses with cracked ice, or serve in a punch bowl with a large block of ice. This makes enough for thirty-two punch glasses.

HOT CHOCOLATE SAUCE

1 1/2 cups sugar
3 tablespoons soft butter
4 ounces melted chocolate
1 cup cream
1 teaspoon vanilla

Combine and stir until dissolved the sugar, butter, chocolate and cream. Boil these ingredients without stirring for seven minutes. Stir in vanilla. Keep the sauce hot in a double boiler. Makes about two cupfuls.

A-P's

1 pound butter
1 pound granulated sugar
3 eggs, unbeaten
1 pound sifted flour
4 tablespoons milk or cream
1/8 teaspoon salt
Nut halves
Powdered cinnamon and sugar
1 extra beaten egg

Cream the butter and sugar, add the unbeaten eggs, one at a time. Add the flour and milk, alternately, and the salt. Chill the dough overnight. Then roll a small amount at a time as thin as possible, on a lightly floured board. Cut with cooky cutters in fancy shapes. Paint with beaten egg and decorate with nut halves. Sprinkle with cinnamon and sugar. Bake in a hot oven (400° F.) for four or five minutes, or until lightly browned. This makes two hundred or more, depending on the size of the cutters.

CHRISTMAS COOKIES

1 pound flour
1 teaspoon salt
2 teaspoons baking powder
1 pound sugar
1 pound butter
1 teaspoon cinnamon
3 eggs, unbeaten
Blanched almonds
Extra sugar

Sift the flour twice with the salt, baking powder and sugar. Mix in the butter, cinnamon and eggs, kneading until a soft dough is formed. Chill well. Then roll it very thin on a well-floured board. Cut with a cooky cutter. Sprinkle with granulated sugar and place one almond on each cooky. Bake six to eight minutes in oven (350° F.). This makes two hundred or more cookies.

BUTTER "S"

1/2 pound butter
8 egg yolks
1/4 pound sugar
1 pound sifted flour
1 lemon rind, grated
1/2 teaspoon baking powder
Beaten egg

Cream the butter, beaten yolks, sugar and rind until lemon colored. Add the flour sifted with the baking powder. Mix well, then take about one tablespoon of the dough in your hand and roll it and shape into an S. Place these cookies on a greased baking sheet but let them stand several hours before baking. Then brush them with beaten egg. Bake in a moderate oven (350° F.) twelve to twenty minutes. This makes four dozen or more cookies.

CHEESE COOKIES

1 package cream cheese
1/2 pound butter
1 cup granulated sugar
2 cups sifted flour
1 1/2 teaspoons baking powder
1/8 teaspoon salt

Cream the cheese and butter together. Sift the flour with the baking powder and salt. Mix well together. Roll very thin on a lightly floured board. Cut and bake in a low oven (275° F.) twelve to fifteen minutes. This makes five dozen or more cookies.

VANILLA WAFERS

1/2 cup butter | *1/2 teaspoon vanilla*
3/4 cup sugar | *1 egg, beaten*
1 cup sifted flour

Cream the butter and sugar, add the vanilla, beat in the egg and gradually add the flour. Drop by teaspoonfuls on a greased baking sheet. Bake in a moderate over (350° F.) ten to twelve minutes. This makes thirty or more wafers.

KISSES

1 egg white | *1/4 cup granulated sugar*
1/4 teaspoon vanilla

Beat the egg white very stiff, add the sugar gradually, then the vanilla. Bake on brown paper in a low oven (275° F.). This makes twenty-five kisses.

ICE BOX COOKIES

1/2 pound butter | *1 egg, beaten*
2 cups granulated sugar | *3 cups sifted flour*
1 teaspoon vanilla

Cream the butter and sugar together, add the vanilla then to the beaten egg. Gradually add the flour until stiff enough to form into three rolls. Put these in the refrigerator overnight. Slice thin and bake in a moderate oven (350° F.) ten to fifteen minutes. Five dozen or more cookies.

ICE BOX COOKIES (Brown)

1/2 pound butter | *1 egg, beaten*
1 cup brown sugar | *2 teaspoons vanilla*
1 cup white sugar | *3 1/2 cups sifted flour*
1 1/2 teaspoons powdered cinnamon

Cream the butter with the two kinds of sugar. Add the beaten egg and vanilla, then the flour sifted with the cinnamon. Mix and form into three rolls. Chill these in the refrigerator overnight. Slice thin and bake in a moderate oven (325° F.) ten to eighteen minutes. This makes five dozen or more cookies.

PECAN FINGERS

3/4 cup butter
4 tablespoons powdered sugar
2 cups sifted pastry flour
1/8 teaspoon salt
2 tablespoons vanilla
1 cup chopped pecans

Blend the butter into the sugar, add the sifted flour and salt and mix thoroughly. Add the vanilla and nuts. Shape into "fingers." Bake about twenty minutes in a moderate oven (275° F.). This makes about three dozen fingers.

NUT COOKIES

1 1/2 cups brown sugar
1 cup butter
2 eggs, well beaten
1 teaspoon baking soda
2 tablespoons freshly made coffee
2 1/2 cups sifted flour
1 cup seedless raisins
1 cup chopped nuts, black or English walnuts

Cream the butter and sugar, add the eggs, then the soda dissolved in the coffee. Mix, then add the flour, raisins and nuts. Drop by teaspoonfuls on a greased baking sheet. Bake ten to fifteen minutes in a hot oven (400° F.). This makes about three dozen cookies.

NUT COOKY BALLS

1/2 cup butter
2 tablespoons sugar
1 teaspoon vanilla
1 cup sifted cake flour
1 cup finely chopped pecans or walnuts
Powdered sugar

Cream the butter, add the sugar and blend well. Add the vanilla then the flour, mix, stir in the nuts. Roll the dough into small balls and place them on a greased cooky sheet. Bake in a moderate oven (300° F.) for forty to forty-five minutes. Remove from the oven and while they are still hot, roll them in powdered sugar. When cooled, roll them again in sugar. This makes about forty cookies.

ALMOND COOKIES

1 *cup shortening*
1 *cup sugar*
2 *eggs, beaten*
2 *egg yolks, beaten*
2 *cups sifted flour*
1/2 *pound almonds, unblanched and ground*

Cream the shortening and sugar together, add the eggs and the yolks, then gradually add the flour, mixing well. Beat in the nuts and then mix and shape into one big roll. Chill overnight in the refrigerator. Slice and bake on a greased cooky sheet in a moderate oven (325° F.) about twenty-five minutes. This makes four dozen small cookies.

JEWEL BARS

2 *cups sifted flour*
1/4 *teaspoon salt*
1 *teaspoon powdered cinnamon*
1/4 *teaspoon ground allspice*
1/4 *teaspoon grated nutmeg*
3 *eggs, well beaten*
2 *cups brown sugar*
1/4 *cup evaporated milk*
1 *cup soft gumdrops, cut into small bits (omit licorice)*
1/2 *cup chopped nuts*

Sift the flour, salt and spices together. Beat the eggs until light then beat in the sugar and milk gradually. Add the flour mixture in thirds, beating until smooth after each addition. Add the candy and nuts, saving a few gumdrops for decoration. Spread the dough in a greased pan and bake in a moderate oven (325° F.) for thirty-five minutes. Remove from the oven and cut into bars. Spread the top with frosting and the rest of the candy. This makes two dozen or more bars.

PEANUT COOKIES

1 pound salted, roasted peanuts
3 tablespoons flour
1 cup sugar
2 eggs, beaten

Mix the flour with the peanuts which have been crushed with a rolling pin. Add the sugar to the beaten eggs and mix with the peanuts and flour. Drop by small teaspoonfuls on a greased cooky sheet and bake ten to twelve minutes in a moderate oven (375° F.). These cookies become very crisp when cold and must be kept in an air-tight container to hold their crispness. They are grand with a fruit drink or cold milk.

WALNUT PEAKS

1 pound finely chopped black walnuts
1 pound granulated sugar
3 egg whites, beaten stiff

Mix all ingredients, form in small peaks and bake on a greased cooky sheet, ten to twelve minutes, in a moderate oven (350° F.). This makes about forty-five cookies.

DATE BARS

1 cup sugar
1 1/4 cups sifted flour
2 teaspoons baking powder
3 eggs, beaten separately
1 cup chopped nuts
1 cup chopped dates
Powdered sugar

Sift and mix the dry ingredients, add the well-beaten egg yolks and then the nuts and dates. Add the egg whites, beaten stiff. Bake about fifteen minutes in a moderate oven (350° F.) When done, turn this out to cool. Cut in narrow strips and roll each in powdered sugar. This makes about three dozen strips.

CORNFLAKE MACAROONS

2 egg whites, beaten stiff
1/8 teaspoon salt
1 cup granulated sugar
1/2 pound dry coconut
1 teaspoon vanilla
3 cups cornflakes

Beat the egg whites, add the salt and then the sugar and other ingredients. After the cornflakes are in the mixture, if the dough is too wet, add more cornflakes. Pinch into little cones or piles on a buttered pan. Bake in a hot oven (425° F.) about five minutes, until browned. Let stand in the pan to cool. This makes four dozen or more.

CHINESE CHEWS

3/4 cup sifted flour
1 teaspoon baking powder
1/4 teaspoon salt
1 cup sugar
1 cup chopped dates
1 cup walnuts
1/2 cup shredded coconut
2 eggs, well beaten

Mix all the dry ingredients, then add the nuts, dates, coconut and well-beaten eggs. Add the vanilla. Spread the mixture about one-half inch thick in a buttered pan. Bake in a moderate oven (350° F.) ten to fifteen minutes. Remove the pan from the oven, cut the cake in strips while still warm and roll the pieces in granulated sugar; or roll into balls, then into sugar. This makes four dozen or more.

CHOCOLATE CRISPIES

2 squares bitter chocolate, melted
1/2 cup butter
1 cup sugar
2 eggs, beaten
1/2 cup sifted flour
1/2 teaspoon vanilla
1/2 cup finely chopped nut meats

To the melted chocolate, add the sugar, butter, eggs, flour and vanilla. Mix well and spread in greased pans. Sprinkle with ground nuts. Bake fifteen minutes in a hot oven (400° F.). Cut into squares when warm. This makes two dozen or more pieces.

CHOCOLATE DROPS

1/4 pound chocolate
1 can condensed milk
1 pound dry coconut
1/8 teaspoon salt
1 teaspoon vanilla

Melt the chocolate, add the milk, coconut, salt and vanilla. Mix well. Form into balls and place on a lightly greased baking sheet. Set this pan on the bottom of the oven five minutes, then five minutes on the shelf. Have the oven moderate (350° F.). This makes two dozen drops.

SPRITZGEBACKENES

1 1/2 *cups shortening*
1 *cup sugar*
3 1/4 *cups sifted flour*
5 *egg yolks, beaten*
1/2 *lemon, juice and grated rind, if rind is liked*

Cream the shortening and sugar, add the beaten yolks, then the lemon juice. Add the flour, beating well, until stiff enough to drop by teaspoonfuls onto a greased cooky sheet. Bake in a moderate oven (350° F.) twelve to fifteen minutes. These may be decorated with a candied cherry or piece of candied pineapple before baking.

MARZIPAN

1 *pound almonds, blanched, then finely chopped*
1/4 *pound almond paste*
1 1/4 *pounds powdered sugar*
2 *egg whites, unbeaten*

Blanch the almonds and dry them. Grind them fine and mix with the almond paste. Sift the sugar and add. Mix and knead to a stiff paste with the unbeaten egg whites. Roll with the hand on a board sprinkled with powdered sugar. Cut in pieces the size of a walnut and roll each one-half inch thick. Bake twenty minutes in a moderate oven (325° F.). This makes four or five dozen pieces.

ALMOND MACAROON CAKES AND FROSTING

1/2 *cup shortening*
1/2 *cup sugar*
1 *egg, beaten*
2 *cups sifted pastry flour*
1/4 *cup chopped almonds*

Cream the shortening and sugar together, then add the egg, flour and chopped almonds. Put the dough on a well-floured board. Knead it a little, roll it rather thin and cut with a cooky cutter. Lay these on a lightly greased cooky sheet. Prepare the frosting:

FROSTING

1 egg, beaten
1 cup sugar
1 tablespoon lemon juice
1 cup finely chopped almonds
Candied cherries, citron or angelica

Beat the egg and sugar together for ten minutes. Add the lemon juice and nuts. Place a small mound of the mixture on top of each cooky. Bake in a moderate oven (350° F.) until the frosting is crinkly. Add bits of candied cherry, citron or angelica to the center of the frosting before baking or afterwards. The recipe makes about three dozen cakes.

LEBKUCHEN

3 eggs, unbeaten
3 eggs, beaten separately
1 pound brown sugar
4 cups flour, sifted four times
2 teaspoons baking powder
1/4 pound shaved citron
1/2 pound grated almonds
Confectioner's sugar

Combine the whole eggs, egg yolks, brown sugar, flour, baking powder, citron and almonds. Mix, then roll one-half inch thick on a lightly floured board. Cut into shapes. Bake on a greased and floured cooky sheet, ten to twelve minutes, in a hot oven (400° F.). After baking, ice with white icing made with three egg whites and confectioner's sugar. This makes four to six dozen cookies.

BUTTER GEBACKENES

1/2 pound butter
1/2 pound sugar
3 eggs, beaten
1 pound sifted flour
1 teaspoon baking powder
1 teaspoon powdered cinnamon
2 cups chopped almonds

Cream the butter, sugar and eggs. Add the flour sifted with the baking powder and cinnamon. Mix and add the nuts. Roll thin on a lightly floured board. Cut into shapes.

Bake in a hot oven (400° F.) twelve to fifteen minutes. This makes four dozen or more.

REFRIGERATOR ROLLS

1 *cup scalded milk*
1 *yeast cake*
1/2 *cup lukewarm water*
2/3 *cup shortening*
7/8 *cup sifted flour*
1/2 *cup sugar*
1 *teaspoon salt*
1 *cup mashed potatoes*
2 *eggs, beaten*

Dissolve the yeast in the water. Pour the milk over the shortening, sugar, salt and potatoes. When cool, add the yeast. Mix thoroughly and add the eggs. Stir in enough flour to make a stiff dough. Turn it onto a floured board and knead it a little. Place in a greased bowl, cover and set in the refrigerator. About two hours before baking, shape the dough into rolls and let them rise until double in bulk, in a warm but not hot place. Bake in a hot oven (425° F.) for twelve to fifteen minutes. This makes a dozen large rolls, two dozen or more small ones. This keeps in the refrigerator four to six days.

TURKEY FILLING (For a large bird)

6 *loaves bread*
1 *pound suet* (*in place of butter*)
2 *onions, ground*
6 *outside stalks of celery with good leaves*
1/2 *bunch parsley, ground*

Cut off the crusts, crumble the bread. (The crusts may be dried and used later for crumbs.) Put the suet through the food chopper, then grind the celery stalks, leaves and the parsley. Combine all ingredients, season to taste with salt, pepper and poultry seasoning. Stuff into turkey before roasting.

LEMON BUTTER

4 *eggs, beaten*
2 *cups granulated sugar*
3 *lemons, juice and grated rind.*

Beat the eggs and sugar to a cream, add the lemon. Cook in the upper part of a double boiler, over boiling water, until it thickens. Pour into glasses and cover. Use the same as marmalade.

HOLLANDAISE SAUCE

1/2 cup butter
2 egg yolks
1 tablespoon lemon juice
1/4 teaspoon salt

Divide the butter in three pieces. Put the egg yolks, salt and lemon juice in the top of a double boiler, over boiling water, and beat with a fork. Add the first piece of butter and cook until the butter is melted, stirring constantly. Add the second piece and when that melts, the third piece. Stir constantly. Remove the pan from the fire as soon as the last bit of butter is melted. Lift the pan out of the lower pan of hot water also. The mixture curdles if overcooked. This makes about three-quarters of a cup of sauce.

AUNT HETTIE'S SALAD DRESSING

4 egg yolks
2 tablespoons butter
1/2 cup sugar
2 tablespoons vinegar
1/8 teaspoon dry mustard
1/8 teaspoon red pepper

Mix all together and cook in the upper part of a double boiler, set over boiling water, stirring all the time. Thin with a little cream, either plain or whipped, before using. Excellent for fruit and jellied salads.

COLE SLAW DRESSING

1/2 cup granulated sugar
1/4 cup vinegar
1 egg, beaten
1 teaspoon butter

Mix the sugar, vinegar and egg and cook until thickened. Add the butter. Remove from the heat, let cool, and mix with mayonnaise to the proper consistency.

CRANBERRY AND ORANGE RELISH

1 quart cranberries
1 whole orange
2 cups sugar

Put the washed cranberries and the whole orange (take out seeds) through a food grinder. Add the sugar. Mix and put in glass jars to keep in the refrigerator until needed. Ready for immediate use.

APPLE SALAD

6 to 8 apples, medium size
2 cups sugar
1 cup hot water
1/2 pound red cinnamon candies
Chopped nuts
Chopped dates

Wash, pare and core solid apples and cook them until tender with the sugar, water and cinnamon candies. When cold, fill the centers with chopped nuts and dates. Serve on lettuce with mayonnaise as any other salad. Apples resemble tomatoes.

ASHEVILLE SALAD

1 can condensed tomato soup
3 packages of cream cheese
2 tablespoons gelatin
1/2 cup water
1 cup mayonnaise
1 1/2 cups chopped celery, green peppers and onion

Bring the soup to boil and add the cheese, stirring thoroughly. Remove from the heat and add the gelatin which has been softened in cold water. Stir in the mayonnaise and other ingredients. This makes one large salad or sixteen individual molds. Chill until firm.

QUICK CRANBERRY SALAD

1 envelope gelatin
1 1/4 cups cold water
2 cups cranberries
1/2 cup chopped celery
1 cup sugar
1/4 cup chopped nuts
1/2 teaspoon salt

Cook the washed cranberries in one cup of the water for twenty minues. Stir in the sugar and cook five minutes longer. Soften the gelatin in one-fourth cup of water, add to the hot cranberries and stir until the gelatin is dissolved. Strain and cool. When the mixture begins to thicken add the celery, nuts and salt, mix with a fork. Return to the refrigerator to become firm. This makes six individual salads, or one large one.

RECEPTION SALAD

1 *package lemon-flavored gelatin*
Juice and fruit 1 *large can crushed pineapple*
2 *packages cream cheese*
1 *small can pimientos*
1/2 *cup chopped celery*
2/3 *cup finely chopped walnuts*
1/2 *pint heavy cream, whipped*
1/8 *teaspoon salt*

Mix the lemon gelatin with the pineapple juice (which has been boiled and allowed to cool). When the mixture begins to thicken add the pineapple and other ingredients in the order given. Chill until firm. This serves twelve.

ENGLISH PLUM PUDDING

1 *dozen tea buns or sweet, plain buns*
1 *quart milk*
1 *pound suet, ground*
1 *pound seeded raisins*
1 *pound currants*
1 *pound citron, sliced in small pieces*
1/2 *pound candied orange peel, sliced in small pieces*
1/2 *pound candied lemon peel, sliced in small pieces*
1 *pound sugar*
6 *eggs, beaten*
6 *apples, ground*
1/2 *pound almonds, ground*
About 2 *teaspoons each of grated nutmerg, powdered cinnamon and mace*
Flour, enough to make stiff batter

Pull the buns to pieces and pour the milk over them to soften them. Grind the suet, apples and almonds. Add the well-beaten eggs to these two mixtures, then the rest of the ingredients and mix well. Then add enough flour to stiffen. Grease cans and molds with well-fitting covers and fill each nearly full. Cover and boil for about twelve hours. Remove from the boiler and take the covers off the molds to let the puddings dry. Replace the lids and store in a cool place till wanted.

OZARK PUDDING

1 *egg*
3/4 *cup sugar*
1/3 *cup flour*
1 1/2 *teaspoons baking powder*
1/8 *teaspoon salt*
1/2 *cup chopped apples*
1/2 *cup chopped nuts*
1 *teaspoon vanilla*
1 *cup cream, whipped*

Beat the egg well and add the sugar, beating until light and creamy. Sift the flour, baking powder, salt and add to egg mixture; blend well. Fold in apples and nuts; add vanilla. Pour into greased, paper-lined dish; bake in a slow oven (325° F.) for thirty minutes. Serve with whipped cream. About eight portions.

PLUM PUDDING SAUCE

2 *cups granulated sugar*
3/4 *cup butter*
4 *egg yolks*
2 *teaspoons vanilla*

Cream the sugar and butter, heat to boiling in the upper part of a double boiler, over boiling water, until the sugar is thoroughly dissolved. Let it cool, then add the well-beaten egg yolks, stirring continuously. Then add the vanilla. Six or more servings.

PUDDING SAUCE

1/2 *cup melted butter*
2 *eggs, beaten separately*
3/4 *cup sugar*

Add the melted butter to the beaten egg yolks. Beat with an egg beater. Add sugar and beat again. Fold in the stiffly beaten whites, add flavoring of choice, such as vanilla, to taste. Four or more servings.

PUDDING SAUCE

1 pint medium cream
4 egg yolks
1 1/2 cups sugar
2 teaspoons vanilla

Whip the cream, not too stiff, add the sugar, egg yolks and vanilla. Serves six.

MINCEMEAT

2 pounds beef (boiled till tender and then ground)
2 pounds seeded raisins
2 pounds seedless raisins
2 pounds currants
1 pound citron, ground
1/2 pound candied lemon peel, ground
1/2 pound candied orange peel, ground
2 pounds suet, ground
4 pounds apples, peeled and ground
2 nutmegs, grated
2 pounds sugar
2 tablespoons powdered cinnamon
1 tablespoon powdered mace
1 tablespoon powdered cloves
3 oranges, juice and grated rind
3 lemons, juice and rind
1 quart grape juice

Mix all together and add the grape juice. Place in crocks or seal in jars and use when desired.

NEVER-FAIL PIE CRUST

(Enough for Two Two-Crust Pies)

1/2 cup boiling water
1 cup lard
3 cups sifted flour
1 teaspoon baking powder
1 scant teaspoon salt

Pour the boiling water over the lard. Beat till cold and creamy. Chill it, if you have time. Sift the flour, baking powder and salt then combine the liquid and sifted ingredients and stir them until they form a smooth ball. Cover the dough and chill it until firm. Roll as for any pie crust. Improves with keeping a day or two in the refrigerator.

CRANBERRY SHERBET

1 quart cranberries
2 cups water
2 cups sugar
2 lemons (juice)
1 tablespoon gelatin or 2 egg whites

If the gelatin is used, soak it in a little cold water and then dissolve in the hot cranberry sauce made by cooking the washed cranberries in the water till tender. Strain to remove the skins. Add the sugar and lemon juice. When cold put it in the refrigerator freezing tray and stir or beat two or three times during the freezing period.

If egg whites are used, omit the gelatin, and freeze the sauce to the mushy stage. Then beat it and fold in the stiffly beaten egg whites. Pour the mixture back into the freezing tray and set it in the freezing unit. Stir several times during the freezing period. Twelve servings.

CHOCOLATE MOUSSE

1 package (6 ounces) chocolate bits
3 eggs
1 tablespoon strong black coffee

Melt the chocolate in double boiler, remove from heat, beat in egg yolks one at a time. Add the coffee, and then the well-beaten egg whites. Pour into sherbet glasses. When hard garnish with whipped cream and a cherry. Four servings.

LEMON BISQUE

1 package lemon-flavored gelatin
1 cup hot water
Juice and rind of 1 lemon
2/3 cup granulated sugar
1 can evaporated milk, whipped
Cookies or macaroons

Mix the gelatin, water, lemon and sugar. Set in the refrigerator to thicken. Whip the evaporated milk (which has been in the refrigerator a few days). Add a dash of salt. Whip the thickened gelatin mixture, then add to the milk. Crumble macaroons or cookies and line an oblong pan. Pour the mixture over the crumbs and cover with more crumbs. Put the pan in the refrigerator to thoroughly chill and set. Ten servings.

DATE DELIGHT

1 pound graham crackers
1 pound chopped dates
1 pound chopped marshmallows
1/2 pound nuts, chopped
3/4 pint cream
Whipped cream

Roll the crackers into crumbs, cut the dates, marshmallows and nuts into small pieces. Mix all together and use enough cream to hold together. Make into a roll and wrap it in waxed paper. Put in the refrigerator overnight. Cut in slices and serve with whipped cream. Eight to sixteen slices.

BREAKFAST CAKE

1 1/2 tablespoons shortening
1 cup sugar
2 eggs, beaten
3 cups sifted flour
3 teaspoons baking powder
1/2 teaspoon salt
1 cup milk
Cinnamon, brown sugar, butter

Mix as for any cake. Spread in three greased cake pans. Sprinkle with cinnamon and sugar and dot with butter. Bake in a moderate oven (375° F.) for twenty to twenty-five minutes.

ORANGE CAKE

1/2 cup butter
1 cup sugar
2 eggs, beaten
1/2 cup sour milk
1 teaspoon baking soda
2 cups sifted flour
1/8 teaspoon salt
1 whole orange, ground
1 cup seeded raisins, ground

Cream butter and sugar, add the beaten eggs. Dissolve the soda in the sour milk and add to the flour and salt. Mix well, adding the whole orange and raisins that have been ground. Bake in two greased layer cake pans, in a moderate oven (350° F.).

Icing to use between layers and on top:

1/4 cup butter
2 cups xxxx sugar
Juice 1/2 orange
Yolk of 1 egg
Grated orange rind on top

Blend all ingredients.

FRUIT CAKE

1 *pound sugar*
1 *pound sifted flour*
3/4 *pound butter*
2 1/2 *pounds currants*
4 *pounds seeded raisins*
1 *pound chopped citron*
1/4 *pound dried orange peel (use the candied peel)*
1/4 *pound flour, to be mixed with all fruit in the bowl*
10 *eggs, beaten separately*
1/2 *cup grape juice*
1 *tablespoon powdered cinnamon or any spice to taste*

Mix all together and bake in greased loaf pans, three hours in a slow oven (250° F.). This makes six two-pound cakes. If baked in smaller pans, bake only two hours.

SPICED WALNUTS

1 *cup sugar*
5 *teaspoons water*
1 *teaspoon powdered cinnamon*
1 *teaspoon vanilla*
2 *cups English walnut halves*

Combine the first four ingredients and bring to boiling. Remove from the heat and add the nuts. Stir a few minutes. Lift the walnuts from the syrup, separate them and let them dry on waxed paper.

CANDIED GRAPEFRUIT

Cut grapefruit in halves. Scoop out the fruit with a sharp spoon or knife. Soak the rind in warm water for two to four days, changing the water from time to time to keep it warm as much of the time as possible. Drain and cut the rinds in slices with the scissors, or cut in shapes with small cooky cutters. Boil the rinds until tender in several changes of water. When tender put the rinds in a syrup made of two parts of sugar to one part of water. Boil until the rind is quite clear. Lay the pieces on a platter until they are dry and then roll them in sugar.

SUGARED APRICOTS

1 pound dried apricots — *1/2 cup sugar*

Wash the fruit, drain it and place it with the sugar in the upper part of a double boiler. Steam it for one hour over boiling water. Then drain it and put it out on waxed paper and let it dry overnight. Roll in sugar the next day.

NEVER-FAIL FUDGE

1 pound confectioner's sugar
4 squares chocolate
1 small can evaporated milk
2 tablespoons butter
Vanilla
1 can marshmallow whip

Combine all ingredients and boil for ten minutes. Remove from the heat and beat in the marshmallow whip. Pour into a lightly buttered square pan. Let it cool and become firm. Cut in squares.

CARAMELS

2 cups white sugar
1 cup light or dark corn syrup
3 cups milk
1/4 teaspoon salt
3 tablespoons butter
1 teaspoon vanilla
1 cup chopped nuts

Cook the sugar, corn syrup and one cup of the milk until it forms a soft ball when a little is dropped into a cup of cold water. Then add another cup of milk and cook again till it forms a soft ball in cold water. Then add the last of the milk, the salt and butter and cook until it forms a soft ball in cold water. Add the vanilla and nuts and pour onto a buttered pan. Let stand for about six hours before cutting into squares.

BUTTERSCOTCH

2 cups white sugar
1/2 cup corn syrup
1/2 cup boiling water
4 tablespoons vinegar
1/2 cup butter
1/2 teaspoon salt

Cook the sugar, corn syrup, water and vinegar together until soft ball is formed when a little is dropped into a cup of cold water. Then add the butter and salt and pour into a buttered pan. Cut before it gets too hard.

13 . . . The Spirit of Christmas

IN A WONDERFUL WAY the legends, customs and traditions of many lands and peoples are combined in our celebration of Christmas. This explains the great variety of its symbols. Stars and angels, trees and wreaths, bells, candles and yule logs mean Christmas in America. Charles Dickens's *A Christmas Carol* is a favorite story of the season. Nearly every child from the cradle onward also hears and loves that most famous of all Christmas poems, *A Visit from Saint Nicholas,* first told by Dr. Clement Clarks Moore to his children in 1822 and first published by *The Troy Sentinel* on December 23, 1823.

We have borrowed and adopted carols from many lands, especially from France and England. The Christmas tree came first from Germany, the significance of the mistletoe originated in ancient Britain, the reindeer which carry Santa Claus through the sky are from far northern lands.

It is this universality that permits all peoples, all faiths and creeds, to share in the happiness and simple joy of Christmas. A Child was born, a star shone bright, and wise men and shepherds brought gifts and reverence to the Babe in the manger. This fundamental of all Christian faith has for many centuries inspired the true celebration of Christmas. It has set it apart from the rest of the year as a time of giving and goodwill and fellowship among men.

Sometimes it seems that Christmas has become too commercialized, too much a shopping season, too much a time for material things. Yet everyone may find a place in his heart, and in his home, for its true spirit. Love and kindness and the happiness one person may give to another, these are the real objectives of our Christmas festivities. Therefore a card of greeting, a spray of evergreen from one's own garden, a visit to an old friend may bring more happiness than a costly gift.

It is at this season that we may recover a sense of values, so easily lost in the world's daily turmoil. By observing Christmas properly we discover what is precious and what is unimportant. We may learn, too, that happiness is always within our reach, since it depends on that which comes from within and above, not on the things of this world.

All over our country there have grown up new ways and customs of keeping Christmas, founded on those of long ago. At Bethlehem, Pennsylvania, a great Christmas star set high on a mountain side is visible for miles around, sparkling with welcome from a city named for the little village where the Christ Child was born. Close by at Allentown and Nazareth, the Pennsylvania-Germans, more commonly called the Pennsylvania-Dutch, go to infinite pains to set up a *Putz,* or Christmas village, a landscape of buildings, trees and animals. Sometimes a whole room or the main part of the house is occupied by these elaborate displays. Creches or cradles are constructed with the traditional characters in life-size. These also appear in miniature in many homes.

Increasingly the cities and towns of the United States are celebrating Christmas by decorating streets, public buildings and squares. In my opinion displays are usually most attractive, in the small communities, where there is more personal interest and pride in them. It is one of my own Christmas pleasures to journey, when possible, to such towns as Bethlehem, Allentown, Emmaus, Nazareth,

York, Lancaster, Reading or Gettysburg, to see the beauty and variety of the decorations.

Yet the proper place for keeping Christmas is in the home. Here each member of the family may contribute something to the celebration and every decoration may be fondly contrived. It is the purpose of this little book to make the decoration of the home for the happiest season of the year a real labor of love.

This calls for originality, patient self-criticism and an open mind for new ideas and fresh material. It means that you will often think of Christmas through the year, while walking, traveling, working in the garden or enjoying the infinite beauties of nature. From the world without, many lovely things may be taken indoors in mid-winter as beautiful and fragrant gifts to the Child whose birth Christmas celebrates.

For a long time I have enjoyed more than any other of my lectures the talks and demonstrations which have supplied the material for this small volume. I hope now that you will find as much delight in carrying out these suggestions as I have had in presenting them. I hope, too, that you will experience real creative joy as each year you MAKE YOUR OWN MERRY CHRISTMAS.

Index